PRAISE FOR

Two Minus On

"There are times in life when we are presented with unforeseen challenges that feel so overwhelming, we just want to shut down and hide. In those moments we have a choice, to go toward the light or stay in the darkness. Kathryn shows us her deepest sadness, and her heroic struggle to get her life back. Her book shows how she recognized that there is life after grief and suffering, and to remember that happiness is always a choice, one we *do* have control of."

—JENNIFER PATE GILBERT, founder of *Save the Date* and author of *I Never Promised You a Goodie Bag*

"Kathryn Taylor's book is a gift to anyone who is divorced and feeling hopeless, because she illustrates through her own story of suffering, disillusionment, and eventual triumph that divorce is not the end. Her words underscore the fact that good things can and do come out of the bad if we let them, and there is every reason to hope for a happy future, despite the devastation. I highly recommend that anyone who is divorced and feeling alone in their fight to survive read *Two Minus One* to gain encouragement, clarity, and hope."

—LISA DUFFY, author, speaker, and divorce recovery coach

"From the words that came out of the blue—'I'm done with our marriage'—through the desolation, heartbreak, and steps toward healing, Kathryn Taylor opens her heart and soul to take us on her journey of recovery. With resilience and grace, she reminds us that no matter what life throws your way, you can reach down and bring up the courage to not only go on but grow."

—VIKKI STARK, author of *Runaway Husbands: The Abandoned Wife's Guide to Recovery and Renewal*

"*Two Minus One* is a story of a woman who finally allows herself to love again, only to have everything taken from her by a man who becomes a stranger overnight. On these pages, Taylor captures the confusion, grief, and outrage that occur when one partner inexplicably walks away, and beautifully describes how she learns to stand on her own two feet. This is a powerful story of grace and resilience."

—TAMMY LETHERER, author of *The Buddha at My Table: How I Found Peace in Betrayal and Divorce*

"In her memoir, *Two Minus One*, Taylor offers a poignant and well-crafted account of what it is like to be sixty years old, believing you are happily married one day, only to discover the next, having missed all of the clues, that you've been abandoned. This is certainly a story that demonstrates the powerful ways in which love is blind. This is a human story, one of vulnerability, insight and resilience. Highly recommended."

—DIANE POMERANTZ, PHD, author of *Lost in the Reflecting Pool*

Two
Minus
One

Two
Minus
One

A Memoir

Kathryn Taylor

SHE WRITES PRESS

Published 2018
Printed in the United States of America
ISBN: 978-1-63152-454-7 pbk
ISBN: 978-1-63152-454-7 ebk
Library of Congress Control Number: 2018947868

For information, address:
She Writes Press
1569 Solano Ave #546
Berkeley, CA 94707

Book design by Stacey Aaronson

She Writes Press is a division of SparkPoint Studio, LLC.

Names and identifying characteristics have been changed to protect the privacy of certain individuals.

Author's Note

This is the true story of my personal journey through unexpected divorce and healing. Only my feelings, perceptions, and interpretations are represented. They were all I had.

For my daughters, Brittany and Erin,
who have been my lifelong inspiration,
as well as the motivation for everything I have accomplished.

And for Robbie,
who has stood beside me throughout my journey wherever it has led.

"You can't control what may happen to you in this life, but you can control who you want to be after it happens."

—JENNIFER GILBERT,
I Never Promised You a Goodie Bag

CONTENTS

༺

Preface

"The only people worthy to be in your life are the ones
that help you through the hard times and laugh with you
after the hard times pass."

—ZIAD K. ABDELNOUR

From an early age, I imagined myself as a teacher yet also envisioned myself as a writer. In junior high school, I sent for a writing test from the back of a magazine, and my efforts resulted in positive comments and encouragement to continue to write. Of course, those who produced the test likely had a writing school that could polish and improve my skills for an extra investment that could be accomplished in several easy payments.

Once, in my twenties, I submitted a short story to a women's magazine. Having long ago forgotten the content, I do recall one thing: it was considered lacking in depth and scope and was therefore quickly yet kindly returned.

Throughout my thirty-year professional career in education, others urged me to write books for children—either age-appropriate fiction or curricular products to enhance a mandated program. But as a single, working mom, I never seemed to have any time to initiate such a project.

Frankly, while I had little trouble with using words, either verbally or in writing, I questioned my ability to do the research required for a nonfiction text. I also lacked the confidence and fortitude even a short book of fiction would require, and steered away.

Until one spring day my life was unexpectedly and forever changed by a personal experience so profound that I found myself at a loss and unable to function. During that time, a friend and former professional colleague asked if I had written yet. I gave my excuses as outlined above. Through my tear-choked sobs—and several glasses of wine—my friend suggested that perhaps it was time. I wouldn't have to research this story—I was living it. She was right. That night, the seed was sown. If everything really does happen for a reason, at that point in my life, perhaps the reason was to push me past the last of my fears and finally force me to sit down to write my story. In doing so, I would ultimately discover that I was not the vile and despicable person my husband attempted to portray.

Prologue

"Never tie your happiness to the tail of someone else's kite."

—BETH HOFFMAN, *LOOKING FOR ME*

*T*ELL ME THE STORY OF US," I SAID QUIETLY, AS WE lazed with coffee and the Sunday paper.

There was no response, and I had expected none. Ours was a story of poor timing, conflict, and pain, as well as romance and joy. So, turning to face him and snuggling even closer, I asked him again. I was confident he would tell me the story I cherished and could never hear often enough. He would tell me—he always did. For his love for me was so deep and selfless, and my need for confirmation and connection so strong, that, even when the edges of pain and loss were always in the retelling, the happiness we had found together was the true story and real strength.

And so he began:

"Once upon a time . . ." This was my favorite part and the way I always asked him to start. It was the only suitable opening for the fairy-tale love we had and the life we were living.

He went on: "A most beautiful mother and her two beautiful daughters arrived in my town, the school of my children, and my life. I was instantly intrigued, and I knew I had to know her. . . ."

Of course, it wasn't a fairy tale—no life is—but we were both giving marriage a second chance, both committed to making it last a lifetime, benefiting and enriching each of us—

the icing on the cake. We communicated openly and honestly in "state of the union" discussions about health, finances, sex, plans, and dreams. We awoke each morning with smiles on our faces. Both of us were filled with gratitude for our good fortune. We had healthy and responsible grown children, good health, solid finances, no elder-care responsibilities, and the ability to shape our days and lives as we saw fit—or so I thought.

CHAPTER ONE

Second Chances

"Lessons in life will be repeated until they are learned."
—FRANK SONNENBERG

*A*S IS OFTEN THE CASE WITH LOVE STORIES, OURS did not begin as love, or even friendship. It just seemed Jim was always there, hovering over and around my world. He was nondescript, non-disruptive, a quiet presence constantly at the ready. He was willing to offer anything to assist my daughters and me and to be a part of our lives. He, his wife, and his children seemed to be everywhere we were. Our children were in the same grades, had the same teachers, and participated in the same activities. His daughter routinely slept at my house and mine at his. He and his wife included my older daughter on their family trips to the beach. He included both of my girls on ski trips. If I were grading papers, preparing a grade book, or doing other work-related chores at a basketball or soccer game, he eagerly offered his assistance. He would turn up to help spread mulch, to fix a leak, or to avert a household calamity. Perhaps he was just taking pity on a woman alone. He and his wife were two of only a handful of people who knew that the girls and I were on our own. They lived nearby, so it was easy to stop in and help when help was needed. I gave it little thought. He was just there.

When my daughters and I were forced to move unexpectedly and dramatically downsized our home, his presence became more and more visible and increasingly routine. He would sometimes appear with his wife and children in tow. "We thought you could use some help arranging furniture." At times, he brought only his son and said, "The two of us can easily get that cabinet mounted in the girls' bathroom." Often he came alone, helping to ease a difficult transition. He restored sanity when the washer, dryer, and refrigerator did not fit into the kitchen. He was there when the TV needed to be lifted, when flooring needed to be laid in the attic, when shelves needed to be built in the garage and closets. He spent weeks planning and erecting a fence to keep an errant dog from getting loose and causing trouble in the neighborhood. He seemed always eager and willing whenever a need arose. He provided comforting words—"This isn't as overwhelming as it seems"—and a strong back. He volunteered in my classroom, arriving at school to read to my students or help them understand, through movement, balls, and a light, what it really meant for the planets to rotate around the sun, and they seemed to clearly understand his method of presentation. But, frankly, aside from when he was there to help or when I was faced with a problem I knew he could help solve, I rarely gave him a second thought.

They happened slowly, over time—tiny actions and behaviors imperceptible both to me and to those around me. Perhaps I was just unaware. Involvement with someone was certainly not on my radar. However, a friendship was developing, as we worked together so often. He began to share some of the frustrations he was experiencing at work. He lamented, "My career seems to be stagnating at a time when I'm preparing to retire." Issues he was facing at home came up as well. He told me, "My wife and I are growing increasingly distant as the kids near the end of high school and prepare to leave for college. I feel we are not working toward the same goals. Perhaps we never were."

OUR FRIENDSHIP TOOK on new meaning the evening Jim, and his wife, Marge, invited me out to dinner for my birthday at a newly opened Japanese steakhouse, insisting it would be their treat. He described his upcoming vacation with his son. "We're planning a week in Vermont over spring break, while Karen is in France for a semester abroad. The snow should be ideal, and the black-diamond slopes in Killington are a real challenge."

I was not a skier, yet I found myself awed by his enthusiasm and wondered what Vermont in the springtime would be like, as it was one place I had never visited.

Marge's voice broke through my momentary reverie as she said, "You and the girls really should join the guys on the trip."

"Are you sure that kind of arrangement is appropriate?" I asked.

She remained adamant: "It's a perfect opportunity for a getaway, and our teens will have a wonderful time together."

Far overdue for a diversion for myself and my girls, and confident that we would be traveling with a trusted friend at affordable prices, we began planning. There would be a play and sightseeing in New York City, as well as a quick visit to Montreal (my younger daughter had a goal of collecting thirteen countries' stamps in her passport before she completed high school). The itinerary was quickly finalized, all were excited, and the trip was soon under way.

Before the car was even fully loaded, Lemonhead candies that had been spilled had to be cleaned out, a forgotten ski jacket retrieved, and seating arrangements determined. Once we were on the road, all passengers settled in quite comfortably and easily assumed the atmosphere of a routine family outing, with companionable banter in the backseat and traffic observations and updates in the front.

The visit to New York proceeded flawlessly, as teens and adults grouped, paired, and regrouped for planned and spontaneous activities. A side trip to the world's largest kaleidoscope was a humorous diversion on the way to Vermont. Skiing was disappointing—the weather was unseasonably warm and the snow slushy—but I was undeterred, as I had brought a swimsuit and sunbathed contentedly by the pool. A quick trip to Montreal, and we were headed back and settled into the thirteen-hour return drive. The backseat was often quiet while our worn-out teens dozed. Glancing back at them, I commented, "It appears the trip was a complete success."

He nodded and gave me a rare smile. "Successful from our perspective as well, I hope."

The two of us settled in and cheerfully continued to engage in animated and inconsequential conversation during the remaining hours of the trip.

Still, I never really saw it coming. I was focused on assimilating myself and my daughters into a new community. He was still a married man, and I was thrilled with my unfolding new life. My daughters were well adjusted, nearly grown, and delightful young women. I was mastering my profession in a new environment. I had friends, a network, and a home I could afford. My income was inching up and providing me with a growing, albeit modest, investment portfolio. For the first time in my life, I was beginning to feel truly independent and at peace. I had no interest in or room for a relationship in my life.

However, I soon realized that his perception of our friendship was shifting amid noticeable changes in the dynamics between him and his wife as their relationship continued to disintegrate. He explained to me, "We met in a bar while I was in college. Marriage seemed to be the expected 'next step' for us. Two children quickly followed and were the only thing we shared."

Yes, even to a casual observer, they seemed to be mismatched. I would often hear the whispered comments of friends wondering, "What do you think he sees in her?" during the social situations and gatherings in which I found myself sharing time with them. He had a college education, and a solid and stable work history. He enjoyed reading, photography, skiing, and fishing, and dreamed of traveling and exploring new interests and ideas. He stayed current and interested in a variety of topics, from science and technology to pop culture. She had not attended college, had no consistent job experience or expertise, and, when pushed to work to assist in covering household expenses, chose to babysit at home during the school year. That choice afforded her responsibility-free holidays and summers, during which she could spend the days poolside with only her own two children to monitor. Of her husband, she invariably commented at every gathering, "While he possesses book sense, he is totally without common sense." She made it clear to all that she believed herself to be the partner with the latter.

The overall impression that onlookers gleaned from their public interactions was that he was weak and she was overbearing. Indeed, on occasions when dining out was the option, she even set the criteria for the selected restaurant. She would frequent only an establishment that accepted a discount coupon she had clipped from the newspaper or received in the mail, and would order no beverage that was not free of charge. Because she controlled the budget and gave him only a limited allowance, which provided him with very little cash, she always took care of their portion of the bill—making him appear impotent.

As these differences persisted and wore down their marriage, his behaviors toward me seemed to change. He would ask me to walk with him after completing a project and became increasingly open in voicing his frustrations and sharing his plans. He conveyed specifics of ongoing conversations they had shared. "We always intended to divorce once the kids were finished with high school. Now that it's time to leave, she's refusing to let me out. If I fight it, what damage will be done to my relationship with my children? Women always seem to receive the support through divorce, while men receive the blame."

I offered an occasional comment—"The process of divorce is never easy"—but mostly I just listened. He began to share more personal details of their relationship, about what transpired in their bedroom, which I found uncomfortable and disconcerting to hear and suggested he keep to himself.

Shortly after that, he was at my house one day, when he suddenly announced, "I will be leaving my wife and moving in here to live with you."

Unaware that he had concocted a scheme anything like what he had just stated, I stood frozen as I tried to breathe and formulate a reply. Finally, I carefully explained, "That is not going to happen." Making every effort to stop the development of a plan such as his, I made it clear to him that I wanted nothing more than friendship after a volatile and unpredictable first marriage and an equally hostile divorce. I had no interest in love or marriage and clearly pointed out the fact that we were very different people from very different worlds. I repeatedly played the alphabet game, listing A–Z reasons a relationship couldn't work for us: I was mobile, passionate, sarcastic, and openly communicative. He was quiet, Southern, and passive-aggressive, and, except for college, had never left the state where he had been born. I was physically active and confident and had a wide circle of friends. He skied only on occasion, was seemingly quite insecure, and had no friends whom he could identify, besides his children. Above all, he was still married.

Never could I have imagined, nor would I forget, his immediate and dramatic response, and the change it would ultimately make in my life: "I love you, and I have infinite patience."

Unmoved and still unconvinced, I reminded him, "Where you want to go is not where I want to be. You're struggling to unravel yourself from a long-term relationship, and you're an emotional wreck as your marriage comes to an end. You've been reduced to inertia on the job and in your personal life. You need to have time to yourself. You need to sort through your life, your needs, and your goals before you even think about moving ahead with someone else. When you're ready, there will be women who will be looking for a relationship and will welcome you into their lives. I *am not* that woman."

Still, he maintained his love for me, as well as his endless patience.

And so time continued to pass and the attachment deepened. As a friend, I found it difficult to abandon him during such a trying period in his life. We spent increasing amounts of time together, mostly discussing the collapse of his relationship and the pain he was feeling as he struggled to end his twenty-year marriage. His concerns focused mainly on the impact the divorce would have on his children. He was especially concerned about his son, who already had a rocky relationship with his mother. When the separation became official and Jim moved into his own apartment, that bond was further strained. Marge was rarely home to provide much-needed stability in her son's disrupted routine. She was instead enjoying a newly established social life and an expanded dating scene. When her son asked her why she was out so often, she responded, "Do you think your father isn't doing the same thing?" Certainly not the type of conversation to ease a young adult through the transition of divorce. Jim talked endlessly of the guilt he internalized about ending the relationship—even though it had been a much-discussed, mutual decision.

Although I experienced additional concerns, these regarding awkward coincidences he shared with my first spouse—similar first names and birth dates—he was far more like my father, with his carefree optimism and happy whistling, and those concerns slowly began to fade. Ease of conversation, comfortable compatibility, and an ability to honestly and openly discuss any topic or concern continued to build between us. We shared an interest in movies, reading, and restaurants. We both enjoyed the beach—any beach—and we continued to allow our friendship to develop. Despite the drawbacks of timing, children, recovery, and doubts, I did enjoy his kindness and attention.

As the months turned into more than three years, I began to consider a romantic relationship with this man. He became an even more prevalent presence in my home and developed an increasingly closer bond with my daughters, and, as I watched their interactions, I began to believe that somehow, this just might work. However, while my daughters had grown accustomed to his presence in our lives over the years, a more comprehensive conversation seemed necessary as the relationship began to shift from one of friendship to one of romantic involvement.

At first when I asked, "What are you feeling about his place in our lives?" a noncommittal "I'm fine with it" came from both of my children.

Trying again, I reminded them, "Involvement with someone was never something I considered. However, given the respect, admiration, and support he displays for all of us, I would like to see where this might go. And I would like your support."

They shared a conspiratorial look, but I was certain I had them on my side as I excused them from the room. Each hugged me close and offered, "I love you, Mom," as she walked away.

When it came to meeting his extended family, I was nervous. I was raised as a Catholic, held a liberal worldview, certainly enjoyed a nice wine, and was quite apprehensive about how my introduction into his conservative, Southern Baptist clan would be viewed. Although he introduced me as his "friend," the knowing looks we got clearly indicated that his relatives were confident he wouldn't have brought me home unless I were more. His mother and siblings bombarded me with questions about how we had met, how long we had known each other, and where I lived.

As I responded to all their inquiries, we moved into the kitchen to share a casual Sunday supper. I needn't have worried about their acceptance, as the barrage of questions was replaced by supportive comments expressing their gratitude and appreciation to me for the change they saw in his demeanor. His siblings observed, "He's cheerful again." Jim's mother commented, "Before now, he never seemed to feel deserving of anything in life but leftovers and always appeared tired, dejected, and timid." All shared that his wife had often publicly belittled him and expounded on the fact that they had never seen him happier. I smiled shyly as the conversation turned away from his previous relationship and returned to less emotional topics, such as the fruits of the season and the ending of yet another school year.

After that, I was included in all family events. We enjoyed holidays, crabbing, and collaborating on plans to build a third beach house. I began to seriously consider the possibility of a relationship with this man whom I perceived as kind, sensitive, attentive, consistent, and financially and emotionally stable— none of which I had ever experienced before. Starting to "bend and sparkle," as a friend commented about my new zest for every moment, I determined to let this story unfold and watch what might happen.

As he healed from his divorce, the kinks seemed to unravel. His boss had appointed him project manager on a new and demanding assignment, and she gave me the job of providing continued support to him as it moved ahead. When it ended and one project led to another, I continued to "have his back" as his career gained momentum and his reputation soared. I was delighted to help in any way I could and was confident he would do the same for me.

He appeared to gain strength in his independence. When we had first begun dating, he had acted awkward and embarrassed by our relationship. I sensed an overriding guilt that he had failed his children by leaving his wife. I wondered why he felt so undeserving. Was it the collapse of a long-term marriage? The fact that he seemed to move ahead so quickly? His wife had already remarried. He never gave me a clear explanation for his behaviors, but often I was deeply hurt. There were the times when he abruptly took me home because one of his chil-

dren called and needed last-minute assistance with transporta-
tion. There was also the holiday outing in Williamsburg, where
we were too far away to be bothered and happily enjoying the
ambience of the Christmas season. We strolled hand in hand
through shops, until he noticed an acquaintance. He quickly
dropped my hand and walked away from me to approach his
friend, without any acknowledgment that he was with me or
any attempt at introductions.

When I later asked, "Why did you not admit you were
with me? Why did you not introduce me to your friend?" he
gave me no explanation. There was only an awkward silence.

However, as the months continued to pass and the pain from
his divorce faded, he became more willing to be seen openly and
publicly as a couple. We began to share quiet dinners in intimate local restaurants. The movies we went to were no longer
in neighboring communities. He introduced me as his "new
friend" to acquaintances of his we happened upon. I planned
and hosted a surprise celebration for his fiftieth birthday and
invited all of his family and work colleagues, as well as some of
my friends who knew of our situation.

He began to explain to his children about our developing
relationship. Unlike my daughters, they seemed to have far
more difficulty accepting those changes. They were less than
eager in their support and struggled to navigate my transition
from parent of a friend and friend of their parents to their father's romantic interest. It was certainly not smooth sailing and
not always forward movement. However, with open communication, counseling, determination, understanding, and several
years, we grew together. He consistently reassured me, "You
can quit waiting for the other shoe to drop; I'm in this for life."

So when he came by to pick me up for dinner on a cold
and blustery evening, got down on one knee, and asked if I

would consider spending the rest of my life with him, I readily agreed. Both of us felt confident and comfortable that this partnership would last forever and prove mutually rewarding and satisfying. We agreed that the blending of our individually gratifying and contented worlds would enhance both of our lives.

We planned a small wedding, to which only the two of us and our four children would bear witness. We reserved a private room in a historic downtown hotel, where we would exchange vows and share a celebratory dinner together. He and I would then spend a night in one of the beautifully appointed suites before we headed to the beach for our honeymoon weekend. Friends planned a wedding reception upon our return, and we settled into a combined and freshened version of my home to begin our marriage.

As is often the case, life got in the way of our plans. Less than a year after the wedding, I was enrolled, after much mutual discussion and consideration, in a master's program and he was on his way to an overseas assignment in Ireland. Despite the complications of our schedules, I frequently flew to Europe and he often flew home. Daily phone calls, routine cards and letters by mail, and Skype also kept us connected, so the hardship of distance, while not the best for starting this new journey together, was lessened tremendously.

My trips were always quite complex to arrange. I was in class all day on alternating weekends and required a special exemption to miss even one session. I worked diligently and as far in advance as possible to submit papers ahead of schedule, so cohorts would not think I was receiving special favors. He had never toured Europe, so, that first spring, I suggested we forgo our tradition of spending our vacation on the sandy beaches of the Florida Keys, Mexico, or the Caribbean. Instead, we decided to enjoy the tulip festival in the gardens of Kuekenhof, Holland, and to visit Amsterdam. We walked the infamous De Wallen in the red-light district, and we toured the hiding place of Anne Frank. He took endless pictures of the stunning flowers and interesting scenery that surrounded us.

He returned home in May for the college graduations of his son and my daughter, and I was able to make two more trips back to Ireland. We traveled the narrow, winding back roads of the north and marveled at the lush green countryside, the thatched roofs, the rocky coastline, and the traffic jams that sheep caused as they were herded across a country road. We explored pubs, drank Guinness, and ate potatoes prepared in every conceivable way. We purchased Irish crystal, linen, and woolen sweaters for ourselves and for others as gifts.

We spent a long weekend in London, where we saw the Changing of the Guard, London Bridge, Buckingham Palace, and Big Ben. We shopped at Harrods and Covent Garden, where we discovered and purchased an antique brass compass. We purchased tickets for the Theatre Royal Haymarket, where we saw a performance featuring Judi Dench.

We enjoyed a visit to Paris and marveled at the beauty of Notre Dame, Sacré Coeur, and Montmartre. We spent time absorbing the treasures in the Louvre and the Musée d'Orsay. We walked the Champs-Élysées, pausing often at outdoor cafés for wine and cheese. The Arc de Triomphe was beautiful at any time of the day or night, and his favorite sight was the Eiffel Tower, whose engineering design and structure intrigued him. We spent time at Versailles and were both awed by the lush structures and gardens.

We flew to Rome in August and toured the Vatican. We tossed coins into Trevi Fountain, climbed the Spanish Steps, and took in every historic sight the city had to offer. We stayed in Florence and visited Ponte Vecchio, where I purchased a coral bracelet. We explored the Uffizi Gallery, saw Michelangelo's *David*, visited all the beautiful chapels, and indulged in fine Italian wine and cuisine. Every moment, every memory, was caught on camera. He would ask a stranger at each stop to snap a photo and freeze all of our special experiences. Observing his enthusiasm and joy during my visits made the struggle of getting there and the fatigue of the journeys well worth the effort.

On the final day of my final trip, we boarded a train from Florence to Pisa, where we would depart on a flight back to Belfast. In typical womanly fashion, I spotted a pair of beautiful sandals, and he insisted I try them on in my size. They fit perfectly, and the last Italian purchase was made. Clutching the package, as well as our carry-ons, we wound our way through security and approached customs to have our passports stamped for departure. We barely made our flight but settled in comfortably for the quick journey back to Belfast.

As his assignment was ending, it would be the last time we would visit Ireland before his final return home in the fall. Throughout the time that he had been overseas, I had been entrusted with an assignment as well: I had been asked to maintain a vigilant watch over our four children, our three pets, and our primary home, as well as a rental condominium and three beach houses. Although all three elderly and ill pets had to be put down during his absence, my work was considered a success. My accomplishment earned me beautiful diamond earrings, which he encouraged me to choose on my own—and which would later be one of the items that remained a constant in my life.

We also learned during that time that there would be a new professional opportunity for him following the completion of his project in Ireland. It, too, would require relocation and would be temporary. It would have a minimum commitment of three to five years and would be only two states away. The location would keep us within easy driving distance of our children, so we could continue to remain active participants in their lives. Again, there was much discussion regarding the positive and negative impacts on both of our careers, our children, and our lives together. While I was not ready to leave teaching, I felt I could not deny him the role the move would provide. I was also unwilling to risk the marital damage that seemed inevitable if I declined to support his relocation and accompany him on the project. After all, we were newlyweds and he had just returned from one long-term assignment without me. The distance and the length of time felt like too large an obstacle and too big a threat to the building of a strong and lasting union.

So, calling upon all my inner strength and personal experience (this would be my sixteenth move), I began the process of retiring from my thirty-year teaching career and preparing to secure a new home, as well as pack up the old one. Thinking I would sell my house, I was expecting to reconnect with the realtor I had worked with on the purchase. I was surprised to hear my husband say, "I would never expect you to sell your home. I know how important it is to you. I understand the security that it provides to you. You have worked too hard for this. I am already asking you to sacrifice enough on my behalf. We will keep it."

Amazed by his insight and generosity, I found that the relocation felt suddenly less daunting. When friends questioned why I wasn't selling and making a "fresh start," I proudly explained his loving gesture. I restructured the packing plans and determined what we would leave behind. Lawn and pest services were kept in place, and the home was left sparsely furnished. The kitchen remained outfitted. His selfless action would provide a gathering place for family and friends on our routine trips back to visit. Holiday celebrations and milestone events would occur there, and the comfort and camaraderie of our blended families could continue to expand as the families themselves grew by virtue of weddings and births.

We had been put in touch with a realtor in South Carolina, so, each day after school, I viewed dozens of homes on my computer. I waded through extensive information on the Charleston metropolitan area. I studied schools, neighborhoods, and shops. We began to narrow down the possibilities. For nearly six months, we made weekend trips between the two states, searching for a place to live. Having moved so frequently, and acutely aware that the real estate market was at a peak, I was cautious in my efforts. There were already whispers of a coming market adjustment, and we did not want to buy high and risk the possibility of being forced to sell low. That situation was a likely possibility, however, as my husband was the only employee not guaranteed a permanent position at the new job site. We were certainly not eager to face financial catastrophe at our age or at this point in our married life together. After so many moves, I was also unwilling to settle for a home of lesser quality than what I had grown accustomed to.

After months of searching and consideration, we had narrowed our search to three areas around Charleston. We focused on the much-sought-after, trendy, and affluent Mt. Pleasant, the more bohemian area of West Ashley, and the sleepy and untouched Summerville. We determined to settle in Summerville, South Carolina. Historically known as Flower Town in the Pines, Summerville was built around a quaint little downtown square filled with shops and friendly people. It boasted that it was the home of sweet tea and hosted a Flower Town azalea festival each spring. It had quality schools, better proximity to his new job, and lovely homes at slightly more affordable prices than the other areas where we had looked. We refined our offer and added options onto the home, and I began to shop for outdoor porch furniture, accent pieces, and a large living room rug to tie together our current furniture and round out our new surroundings.

Six months later, we arrived in our new state, in our new neighborhood, in our new home—knowing not one single person outside his company. Of course, he had his job and the excitement of his new assignment. I had the task of transforming a house into a home and adjusting to retirement. Where my days and life had always felt complete, I struggled now to fill each one. I focused mostly on supporting and encouraging Jim in his new job, perhaps even at my own expense. I was always available when he felt lonely and wanted to meet for a last-minute lunch. I prepared home-cooked meals, which provided comfort when he returned home at the end of the day. I listened with patience and understanding as he aired concerns over the downturn in the economy and its impact on the new job. When he shared his worry that he would lose his job, I immediately suggested, "I can return to teaching."

He offered a rare smile, gave me a gentle hug, and replied quietly, "There are many ways to contribute to a relationship. Working outside the home and bringing in a paycheck is only one. You contribute in so many more vital ways with your support, enthusiasm, and selfless love."

Slowly and deliberately, I strove to fill the void of the loss I felt from the move. I joined the local fitness center, where the women in the classes helped me feel less lonely during my time there. I spent my afternoons watching cooking shows and happily prepared daily dinners at home now that I was not working full-time. We spent weekends dining out and exploring all that our new location had to offer. I worked diligently and eagerly in my new role, having committed to making the marriage even stronger and to creating a fresh start for us in a new place where we were known only as a couple. No skeletons, no past, only a future—together.

It was not always easy. Even planned and anticipated change never is. I no longer had my children, my home, my career, or my network of friends. However, I focused on positive tasks, such as arranging for painters—as well as painting the entire upstairs myself—scheduling deliveries, and following up on new home punch lists.

Each day after my trip to the fitness center, I explored different areas of our new community, attempting to learn my way around. I wanted nothing more than to provide an easy transition and a comfortable haven for my husband when he returned home each day from the grueling pressures of the new job. While the neighborhood and community were quite isolated and different from any of the places I had lived, the neighbors appeared open and friendly and soon embraced us as a couple at frequently occurring neighborhood gatherings. But mostly, we had each other. Until another change shifted our circumstances.

Amid a faltering economy, my husband's situation at the new job site became less and less rosy. Movement of personnel became routine. Attitudes, both business and personal, grew less optimistic, and uncertainty and insecurity became the norm. When the project was completed, there was little need for a project manager. Staying busy and appearing indispensable became the new business model. We reviewed our financial situation and our long-term plans and determined it was undoubtedly a good time to sell my former home. We listed it with a recommended agent.

Eventually, yet another temporary assignment was mandated, three hours from where we had settled. The company would provide housing for him there during the week, and he would return to our home on weekends. He had no choice but to accept if he wanted to remain employed. We were filled with gratitude that the job was so close. It allowed Jim to continue to work at a stimulating assignment, at no additional cost to us, and enabled us to keep our new home—where we had decided to retire. We were becoming so established, we had even begun serious discussions about installing a backyard pool, using the proceeds from the sale of my home.

So the commuting began. Most weekends he would come home; many weekends I would go there. Either way, we made the best of the new situation and enjoyed the spontaneity and romance that long-distance living afforded. More than ever, we anticipated and appreciated cozy dinners on the town, weekend adventures, and quiet moments relaxing together. Until . . .

CHAPTER TWO

✑

Why Are You Telling Me This Now?

"Betrayal—the worst level of hell."

—DANTE

*I*T HAD FELT LIKE ANY OTHER WEEKEND. WHEN HE had come home Friday afternoon, there had been cocktails and conversation on the screened porch. Despite our frequent daily phone calls, we always seemed to have much to catch up on during the days that he was gone. The time we'd shared since his temporary assignment had begun had always seemed too brief. Still, we tried to pack each moment to the fullest and appreciate any togetherness we did have. I would remember that fateful early-April weekend as yet another in a long series of perfect visits, filled with relaxation, laughter, food, fun, and sex.

He seemed a bit more circumspect than usual, but communication had never been his strength. Our conversation centered on the following week's visit to see his dying brother and the severe personnel cuts he was required to make on his new assignment. Although he continued to receive more than adequate pay raises and a substantial annual bonus and was still viewed as an important asset to the corporation, the stagnating economy and defense cutbacks continued to impact the company's workforce and his sense of job security wherever he was located. Little did I know that when I asked at Sunday brunch about his quiet demeanor and he replied, "I'm just preoccupied with work things and planning the week," those would be some of the last words I would ever hear from him.

Our calls and communication the following week were minimal. He no longer phoned each morning at eight to start his day or at lunch to see how I was doing. The calls I initiated to him went unanswered. He left no perky messages to make me smile during his absence or to fill my day while he was away. When I did get through to him, conversation was strained, and he told me, "We'll have plenty of time to talk in the car on the trip to the lake this Friday." I sensed something weighing heavily on his mind but was at a loss about what it was or how I might help.

I continued to busy myself with preparations for the trip while playing out a variety of scenarios in my mind. After all, his last remaining brother was dying of cancer. His had never been a family of outward emotion or open communication, and perhaps the combination of the job assignment, which kept him away from me during the workweek, and the realization that this was indeed the end for his brother was more than he could express or bear.

Friday morning arrived, and it was time for the drive to the lake. This was a trip that, for weeks on end, I had been diligently planning and preparing. It was to be a mini-reunion with his two siblings and their spouses. I had never understood how he could allow so much time to pass without seeing his family. We were routinely in their vicinity when visiting with our children, and I would often suggest we add another day to our trip to visit his brother and sister. However, those were his choices. I had been the one to initiate this time with loved ones unseen in two years, as a last celebration of a life together before the arrival of the death we all knew we were about to confront.

He arrived home early with his weekend bag packed and a distant look on his face. After a quick kiss and a brief exchange of ordinary words about the weather and the distance, I sensed the unsettled feeling I had been experiencing all week descending upon me once again. *What could be bothering him?* I wondered. *Why won't he talk?*

I had already packed my bags and loaded coolers full of the meals I had carefully made for the entire weekend. As we settled into the car and drove to pick up additional ice to keep the food cold, I could see him watching me in my shorts and bare legs— always a bonus for him on a long car trip. Once again, I felt hopeful that, despite the gravity of the situation and the reason for the trip, we would, as we always did, find a way in the hours ahead to discuss the concerns looming over us. We would determine a plan of action and would together overcome whatever this obstacle was and come out on top. After all, during our eight years of marriage, we had faced our share of challenges. We had navigated our way through blending our families, births and deaths, surgeries, a cancer diagnosis, and relocation. Yet we had always found a way to prioritize our relationship as we determined solutions, and always seemed to be even stronger afterward.

Ice purchased, coolers securely in place, and safely on the interstate, heading toward our destination, I knew it was time for me to ask what was wrong. I had learned from years of experience with this man that he would not be the first to speak, and the building tension was as oppressive as the approaching summer heat. Coming directly to the point, I asked, "What's been on your mind?"

It was then, with seven hours of driving ahead of us, that I heard the devastating words that, under any circumstances or in any situation, I never would have expected. The man who had routinely assured me that I could quit waiting for the other shoe to drop, that he was in it for life, and that he loved me more than he loved his next breath declared, "I'm done with our marriage."

Without pause, he went on to tell me that I was mean and he was tired of telling me that I was mean. He stated that I could find an attorney and he didn't want to talk about his decision. "There's no use talking about it because it's over, things aren't as they were, and never will be, and mean and despicable people can't be changed by talk, no matter who's doing the talking."

Where all of that came from, I hadn't a clue. I felt my head spin, and all the oxygen seemed to escape from the vehicle. Had I thought he meant any part of what he was saying, I would have demanded that he either stop the car or take me home. No, I was certain he was striking out at me over fear of his brother's imminent death. After all, we had our "state of the union" discussions, awoke each day with gratitude for the life we shared, and were closer than ever to full retirement for him and a leisurely life of enjoying each other, our children, and our grandchildren. Just weeks before, we had shared our annual beach trip to celebrate our birthdays at our favorite resort. During that time away from responsibilities, he had lavished thoughtful and sentimental gifts upon me and we had experienced many special moments to add to our collection of memories: leisurely walks on the beach, cocktails on the balcony, and meals out at new restaurants. Only the week before, while I'd been in Austin with my friend Robbie for a long weekend, he had called even more frequently than usual to connect and tell me how much he missed me. He was excited to hear of the sights we were visiting and eagerly asked how we were enjoying our trip. The descriptor "mean" had never been any part of those conversations.

My mind raced to review past situations, as I wondered what could possibly have caused such a shift. I had mentioned to him that the huge varicose vein on his leg looked ugly and threatening. When he had checked with his physician, he had been assured it was not a health risk. We had often discussed that his legs were his most distinctive physical attribute. They were naturally sculpted and effortlessly strong as steel. Wondering why he would want to detract from his finest feature, I went a step further. I told him, "I shouldn't have to look at it." And yes, there had been an occasion or two when we had been partying in the neighborhood and I had consumed too much wine. My razor-sharp tongue had reportedly said hurtful, and unremembered, things. Even less forgivable, on those same occasions, I had somehow fallen asleep during sex. Whether from the wine or from lack of interest, I had not provided the outcome for which he had hoped. However, when I had offered to set the wine aside so that no hurt would be inflicted, he had insisted that was unnecessary. He preferred to continue to play the odds. Most times, the wine drinking loosened inhibitions and made me more docile and accepting of any bedroom games he might want to play later in the evening. The gain was apparently worth the risk.

I concluded that something else must be going on. I was still certain it was his brother's illness. Anyone who knew me would scoff at the suggestion of my being mean. Whatever the circumstances, this could not be happening to us—and not on a road trip. Hours remained in the drive, and a deepening silence surrounded us.

At last, we pulled onto the property of the lake house. Although we were both beach lovers and had frequently discussed buying out his siblings and living in one of his beach properties upon retirement, I had always loved this home. It sat on a lovely piece of real estate, unpretentious and rustic, well appointed and warm. The builder who had designed it had lived there himself before selling, and the stone fireplaces, expansive screened porch leading to an upper deck, and spacious bedrooms were always inviting and relaxing. With a large dock and every water toy imaginable, it was an escape beyond our means, but one we always relished when we were invited to spend time there. His brother and sister-in-law stood there, waiting, smiling, and waving. Taking a deep breath, I looked at him and said, "This weekend is not about me or about you. This is about your brother, and it will likely be the last time we see him. We must both set this aside, put on a brave front, and act the part." A noncommittal shrug from him was the only acknowledgment that he had even heard me. Stepping out of the car, we embraced our family, unloaded the supplies, and walked into the house.

The afternoon moved into evening, and his sister and brother-in-law arrived. Again, I had to dig deep for the strength required to engage once more in perfunctory pleasantries, when all I really wanted was to sneak off to a space by myself. I settled uneasily into the group cadence that was the norm for a gathering of the siblings: a discussion of current events (the bombings of the Boston Marathon and the search for those responsible) and beach properties, as well as the typical banter of our family get-togethers. I was praised for my salad and lasagna, and all were comfortably full as we cleaned up the dinner mess and transitioned to the family room and porch to plan for the next day. I excused myself as soon as possible and headed upstairs to hastily end the evening and try to sort through my jumbled feelings and racing thoughts.

Searching for my phone, I texted my dear friend Robbie to share that I had been told my marriage was over. Reflecting thoughts similar to mine, she responded, "It's a weekend of emotion, and much discussion will ensue as those emotions settle."

As I prepared for bed, my tears began to flow. I wondered how and where I would sleep. How would I be able to survive another two days pretending that all was well with my world? Suddenly, he appeared and began to get ready for bed himself. Probing gently, lest I set off another episode of hostility, yet hoping the first had been a huge misunderstanding, I tried again for conversation.

I soon received confirmation that not only was he done, he was "fucking damn done" with our marriage. My tears began to fall uncontrollably and in earnest. Again, reaching for the security of the anchor of the friendship I had known for more than thirty years, I attempted to call Robbie, hoping she could talk me down from the ledge upon which I found myself. But fate was not kind—cell service at the lake was dicey at best. My call did not go through.

My husband took my phone outside to make the call for me. There was still no reception. Suddenly, he was back, getting into bed beside me and reaching for my hand. I cringed and exclaimed, "How can you reach for me when you've just told me you're through with me? Are you hoping everything will change?" As expected, I received no reply.

Once he was asleep, I slid from the bed. Not wanting to move into one of any number of available bedrooms, lest someone else have a difficult night and search for an unoccupied spot, only to find me, like Goldilocks, asleep in a strange bed, I spent the night on the floor of the bedroom closet. Unable to sleep, I watched the sky as it changed from dark to dawn. I replayed again and again what he had said to me in the car and wondered how I had missed the signs.

Showering and peering at myself in the mirror the next morning, I saw the reminders of the night before. I had red-rimmed, puffy eyes, still heavy from lack of sleep, and a nose crusty from crying. Shrugging and knowing I had no alternative but to descend the stairs and blend into the cheerful conversation I was hearing below me, I slowly turned the knob and opened the bathroom door. I was hoping somehow that coffee would help and that no one would notice how I looked, while still wondering how I had possibly arrived at the current hell I was experiencing and how on earth I would ever survive.

Still now, it remains unclear how the remaining two days passed. Meals were eaten, and there was a dinner out. We all worked together to finish a puzzle, and I advanced my sudoku skills with guidance from his brother. There was time on the dock with conversation and adult beverages that only my husband and I consumed. He and I had a moment alone when he spoke to me candidly, telling me, "I don't know how I'll be able to make it through the end of this marriage without you and my brother for support."

Wanting to respond with the cutting remark "Don't do it," I instead hoped this was an opening for explanation. I reminded him, "Our relationship needn't end. I have supported you to new heights personally and professionally over the last eight years; together we've been an unstoppable pair; I know we can work through this together."

I had no luck. He reiterated his determination to terminate our marriage. We each poured a large glass of wine. Side by side, we returned to the family on the dock. It was such a beautiful, storybook setting for the unraveling of our fairy-tale life.

At last, Sunday morning arrived. It was time for cleaning and packing up. Vehicles were reloaded, there was talk of another gathering, goodbyes were said, and we were on our way. The drive home was even worse than the one up. The trip was a total blur of continuous sobbing on my part, which racked my entire being and exhausted both of us. Once more, he reached for me, this time to assure me, "Nothing will change. We just won't be married." His statements transported me immediately back to the moment, and, dumbfounded by his words, I asked for clarification. He replied that he envisioned a world for us of continued family gatherings, children and grandchildren together for milestone events and celebrations, festive holidays, and home-cooked meals, planned and prepared by me. He stated, "We would just be divorced."

Experiencing a moment of extreme clarity, I sat ramrod straight. "What are you thinking?" I asked. "Have you lost your mind? You want to be done with the marriage but want everything to remain the same? How do you imagine that could possibly work?" He did not respond.

When we arrived at our house, too tired to do any more driving, he informed me he would be staying the night.

He had already erected a wall of silence around himself, though I tried repeatedly to break it down. I begged for intervention. I asked for another chance. I claimed full responsibility for poor behavior. I would have said or done anything to return my life to the way it had been only a week before. I appealed to his compassion. "What will I do here alone? I have no job, no network, no future." In fact, I had only recently sold my previous home. "We were here as a unit, and now I'll be completely on my own."

Still, only silence, throughout the house, throughout the

evening. Until the phone rang, identifying his son as the caller. Of course it was I who answered. Thinking there would be news of another grandchild on the way, I soon learned there was no joyful announcement to offset this horrific situation. His son needed help with his insurance company. I stepped in to offer assistance and eventually resolved the issue—mean as I was. The call over, all conversation again stopped and the house was silent.

Try as I might, I realized there was no escaping this. He was determined to end our life together. I texted a friend to cancel an upcoming visit. Praying for a kiss-and-make-up scenario, I spent a sleepless night in the bed beside him. The following morning, as he headed out the door, I said, "Goodbye."

I heard only, "Get an attorney and decide what you want."

As I stumbled back inside, I left the shutters closed to keep the outside world at bay and made my way to the sofa, where the tears began again. *I* have *to be evil. He* says *I am.* I had thought him to be the better half, the one who inspired me always to rise to my best. I had been certain he loved me completely and unconditionally. So if he was done and he said I was to blame, I must indeed be responsible for the destruction of our marriage.

Minutes after his departure, Jim called and asked if he could come back so we could talk. Again, hoping this was all a huge misunderstanding, I quickly responded, "Yes!" I brushed my hair and my teeth and anxiously anticipated the apology that I was certain would come. Instead of begging forgiveness, he reminded me yet again of my despicable behavior. He insisted I had blatantly dismissed his pleas for me to change. Aside from an occasional offhand comment when he had asked, "Can you throw me a bone?" I had heard no such plaintive requests for behavioral change, only repeated reminders of his unconditional and enduring love. I implored him to understand that I had never clearly understood his message. Again, I apologized. Again, I took full responsibility. Again, he was gone.

There were two more trips back over the following weekends, but little conversation. He displayed a noticeable animosity and hostility that I had never seen before. His behavior was so out of character, he seemed a completely different man. I knew there were limited scenarios to cause such change and attempted to discover the reason. I asked, "Is everything still going well on the job?"

A nod.

"Have you started to experience any new health issues?"

A curt "no."

"Have you been seeing someone while you've been away and want to develop a deeper relationship with her?"

A resounding "There is no one else. I don't want to talk about it."

When I asked why he even bothered to return, he replied, "To take care of things—like the lawn." When I reminded him that I was perfectly capable of taking care of things—including the lawn—and had done it on my own for years, his absence became permanent and official.

In a futile effort to maintain appearances, he returned for a prearranged weekend when my daughter and her boyfriend came to visit. That was a huge mistake. He remained distant and aloof in his interactions, and all but he were clearly uncomfortable. He spent a few hours with me, searching for a new car and revisiting a favorite lunch spot—another desperate and unsuccessful attempt to reclaim my quickly vanishing existence in his life—but then, again, he was gone, with no further word.

Far too long, I remained on the sofa, shutters closed, tears falling uncontrollably. Hours turned to days, and days to weeks.

I was unwilling to leave the house. The shame I felt was immense. I had never experienced pain so deep or emotion so raw, and the unexpected loss immobilized me. I was unable to make sense of what was happening to me, or why. Whatever was I going to do? I had no income, no resources, and now no husband. As he knew, I had always been terrified of homelessness, yet it appeared that some variation of that scenario might be a real possibility.

I had never had much appetite for or interest in food, but suddenly my body was unable to process it at all. It seemed to sense when nourishment was on the way; it shut down my digestive system and immediately eliminated anything I had ingested. Without notice, thirteen pounds vanished from my body and clothes hung from my frame.

I did not take calls from my daughters or friends. How could I talk to or face anyone? Who would want to talk to me? After all, according to what I was being told, I had destroyed a perfectly wonderful relationship and man by being selfish and mean. I did, however, occasionally respond to a text from Robbie and explain that I was unable to talk, capable only of tears.

More time passed. After four miserable weeks, I received yet another text from Robbie. This one contained an ultimatum. She would be calling in ten minutes and was willing to listen to nothing but sobbing. She was going to connect. If I did not answer her call, she would send the police to check on my well-being and would then arrive on my doorstep as soon as she could safely travel the distance between us. Unable to ignore her growing concern, I took the call. Immediately, the floodgates opened and the story began to spill forth.

As promised, Robbie arrived from Atlanta a few days later and movement began. The search for a therapist for me com-

menced in earnest. I reached out to my older daughter to research and procure a new vehicle. I had been looking for
months and would now require something that could haul
things, as a second vehicle would no longer be on hand and my
sporty coupe would not suffice.

Surprisingly, when it came time for me to start looking
for an attorney, I reached out to the person I knew least but
admired most: a woman in the neighborhood whom I saw
routinely in day-to-day life and occasionally at neighborhood
gatherings. A woman who seemed to float above the mundane
happenings of our suburban environment. A woman who
always remained friendly but was clearly not bound by the
quotidian occurrences of the people around her. A person
who seemed genuinely committed to making her marriage
and family her top priority and happily did whatever was
necessary to secure and maintain those priorities, with no
concern about what others might think of her choices. A
woman who, while attending a ladies-only gathering of
neighbors, guiltlessly excused herself to return home to share
with her children a long-distance call from her husband, who
was deployed overseas. A mother who, while attending a
couples' event with her spouse, hastily returned home to attend to and console her daughter, who had fallen from her
bike and slid across the pavement. A woman who, when
asked, "How do you manage to keep up the pace when your
husband is gone so much and your children are so active?"
replied, "I have only one shot at this, and it's my commitment
in life." A person with what appeared to be the strongest
marriage I had seen since I had moved to Summerville.

I don't know why I chose to appeal to her or why she listened patiently to my plea. However, coincidentally, her two
closest friends were well-respected attorneys themselves, and

one of them had just been through a divorce. They gave me the names of two candidates who might represent me in this process. I researched both and chose to meet with the one who was my age and who had secured a fair and equitable settlement for the referring attorney who had just finalized her divorce.

That referral afforded me an inroad that enabled me to bypass the wait and delays typically required of a new client. I met with the lawyer the next day. The first thing I noticed when I was shown into her office was how very cold I felt. The air-conditioning was set at a low temperature, and the window was open. Undaunted—and making a mental note to dress in layers for future meetings, until she provided me with a cozy throw from Pottery Barn to keep me comfortable during our lengthy discussions—I sat across the desk from an animated, professional, and welcoming woman.

As I wondered how or where to begin my saga, she suggested, "Just tell the story," and the recent events began to tumble out tearfully. I explained that this was my second divorce and that I wished to avoid the hostility, pain, and expense I had experienced during my first.

Taking notes, suggesting I consider hiring a private investigator, and assuring me that she, too, preferred an amicable settlement, she talked of options, retainers, potential additional costs, and a payment plan. She walked me gently from her office to my vehicle and reminded me to drive safely on my way home.

After reviewing and discussing this information with Robbie, I took two crucial steps. I called the company holding the one credit card I had and significantly raised my available credit limit to cover legal fees. I then called the attorney's office to schedule another appointment. I returned the next day, signed the required papers, swiped my credit card for the retainer, and headed home again to await the packet of information that would guide me through the steps of the divorce process, as well as the monthly statements of services that I would shortly begin to receive. I felt tremendous relief after accomplishing such an important task. So, bolstered by the added strength and support I derived from Robbie's presence, I continued moving forward.

I scheduled doctors' appointments to test for STDs and check on my general health. I had an old crown replaced and purchased new prescription sunglasses while I still had access to two insurance companies to cover costs. I composed and sent letters and messages to children, family, and friends about the restructuring of my marriage. Early communications were deliberately vague and elusive, as it was unimaginable to me that he would really end our relationship because he had determined that I was mean. I explained that some unexpected issues had arisen that needed further examining and discussion.

As more time passed and he remained unyielding to my requests for communication, I explained that we would take time apart to step back and reexamine the direction in which we were headed. Finally, as I realized he had meant it when he said, "The marriage is over," I explained to others that, although I was confused by the decision and would need some time to sort through the situation, we had, sadly, agreed to terminate our marriage. Both of my daughters called immediately, asking, "How can we help? What do you need?" I received no acknowledgment from either of his children.

Having already accomplished so much, I had a bit of time to partake in activities during the annual Spoleto Festival of music and art, which allowed me to feel almost human for the first time in more than six weeks. Robbie and I squeezed in a little shopping at my favorite boutique, and I purchased a lovely pair of pajamas to mark the passing of my first wedding anniversary spent alone. Even with Robbie's encouragement and amid all the festival fare, I still could not keep food down; however, I believed that venturing out at all was a great start—and I would take a gain wherever possible.

Knowing that I would need continued support after Robbie's departure, I determined to spend time at the beach. I was still part owner of three beach houses, and the ocean always restored my sense of calm and returned me to center. After the beach, I would drive on to see my daughters. I had no plan for my time off; I wished only to regain my focus and perhaps lick my wounds. Food was not necessary. I spent my days soaking up the sun and walking along the familiar contours of the comforting landscape. I collected the few shells that were available and listened to the breaking waves, as I had done for so many years at this very spot. I visited favorite shops where I purchased nothing and restaurants where I was unable to eat.

He had told me that I had anger issues, although he had never mentioned any such patterns—anger-related or otherwise—prior to his announcement that he was leaving. While there, I read a book on anger management and quickly realized that I had no anger issues whatsoever—he had been wrong. I tried several times to connect with him in yet another attempt to resolve what I still considered a misunderstanding. He was still unwilling to talk. My niece, who lived nearby, brought her family to visit for a day, and I watched as they enjoyed Subway sandwiches on the beach. The children were a happy diversion, and I treated them all to barbecue before they headed back home at the end of the day.

After a week at the beach, it was time to continue north to my daughters for their support. I knew it would be a difficult visit for all of us as we addressed this unexpected loss. He had been a reliable and consistent presence in our lives for thirteen years. At times, because of his calm demeanor and close proximity, he seemed even closer to them than their own father. He had helped both of them settle into dorm rooms and moved them into numerous apartments and homes. He had helped with homework, offered advice on school and home loans, and attended graduations and weddings. However, they set aside any questions they had to offer their allegiance and support to a mother in desperate need. They reminded me, "If he has opted out, there is nothing you can do to opt him back in." They wrapped loving arms around me and encouraged me with supportive words. "What can we do to help? Stay as long as you want! We had no clue." They provided noisy distractions from my pain as they insisted, "You have to eat something" and escorted me throughout town for bar-and-restaurant hopping.

While visiting, I received two unexpected and disturbing text messages. In the first, he asked me to call and catch him up on the girls' lives. I reminded him that he had their contact information and could catch up on his own. I also suggested to him that he was not a priority in their lives at that moment.

The second text was even more bizarre and upsetting. In it, he voiced his confusion at my disbelief and sense of betrayal when he ended our relationship. After all, his dissatisfaction had been ongoing for years and shouldn't have come as a surprise to anyone.

Years? I had retired, relocated, and just sold my home. Would I have done any of that if I had known for years that he was unhappy?

Fortunately, he was a state away and I was empty-handed. If he had been near, I envisioned myself wielding a baseball bat at his head and taking great pleasure at the sight and sound of the splat after impact.

Yes, perhaps I was indeed mean.

I texted him and suggested that he remove his belongings while I was away. This story was over.

Unheeding of my daughter's suggestion to extend my stay, I decided it was time to return home. While I was certainly in no hurry to get back to an empty house, I felt as if I had burdened my daughters enough. It was time, at least briefly, to face the new reality of my life. Grateful I had made the trip safely, and turning into my driveway, I retrieved my mail, only to be met by a neighbor walking her dogs. This woman was accustomed to my frequent travel and vagabond ways, but my unexpected and lengthy trip away had surprised her. Maintaining a constant flow of conversation, she asked about the fun I had experienced on my vacation. For the first time, the story tumbled out to someone other than those closest and most trusted in my life. My neighbor expressed the same shock as I myself had experienced. "You two? Who would ever have imagined you wouldn't be a forever thing? He adored you."

I had thought the same myself. Again, grief overwhelmed me. As I entered my home, I wondered again how I would ever survive this ordeal.

CHAPTER THREE

⟨⟩

Time for New Pillows

"You have everything it takes, but it will take everything you have."
—UNKNOWN

*A*FTER I RETURNED FROM THE BEACH, SUPPORT continued in the form of daily phone calls from my older daughter and Robbie, as well as scheduled visits to and from both. I was never left by myself for longer than four weeks. However, right now, I was once again on my own. As I walked into my home after my time away, I immediately sensed a difference. I was totally alone and would continue to be that way. No one would arrive on Friday afternoons eager to see me and share quality time. No one would want to linger Sunday mornings, postponing the time he would have to be away.

Still immobilized by unexpected betrayal and grief, I moved through my days in a zombie-like trance. Listlessly wandering from room to room, I had little interest in anything beyond surviving each day. Memories continued to flood my mind. I could think of nothing more than the fact that he was gone and I was alone. I was certain that if anyone appeared at my door, I would look even more pathetic than I felt. I experienced a sudden memory of the stinging words he had directed at me on the trip, and, in an unexpected moment of emotional strength and defiance, I knew I had to do something. So, two months after his departure, I began my first round of purging, in the hope that I might fool myself into thinking I could return to a normal state.

First to go were the bed pillows—an easy way to eliminate something we had shared. I quickly disposed of them and bought new ones. I thoroughly washed all of our bedding and sent our king-size down comforter to the dry cleaner. I purchased new bed linens and towels. I had erased his smell from my bedroom. Feeling quite smug and savoring the movement and sense of accomplishment, I removed all pictures of the two of us from their frames and tore them to shreds. He was done? Well, so was I.

With the help of physically strong friends, I hauled the last of his furniture into the garage. Awaiting pickup were the very few items he had contributed to our marital home. With that, I moved another reminder of our shared life out of my direct sight as I continued my effort to make sense of the situation in which I found myself. I gave a display cabinet he had wanted for a birthday to a neighbor. I cleaned and sorted shelves, tools, and debris in the garage. I presented to another neighbor the brand-new table saw and stand that my husband had coveted and I had purchased. I donated gloves, sprinkler valves, and a spreader to the man who mowed my lawn. I sold all metal of value.

Room by room, drawer by drawer, closet by closet, I whisked away memories and reminders of an old life. I shredded boxes of cards from him and letters he had written to me. I collected his toiletries and threw them away. When I opened his nightstand, I was confronted with the adult toys we had accumulated. I ignored my typical sense of environmental responsibility, removed the batteries from each—after all, I did live in a hurricane area, where extra batteries were always needed—and put the items directly into the trash. I sorted through my jewelry box and removed for sale pieces of jewelry he had given me. Oddly, I lacked the emotional strength to face the prospect of selling those objects on my own. I needed support from Robbie, on her next visit, to go to the jeweler, initiate conversation about the need to sell the items, and help me to complete that process.

Several times, I sorted my own clothing. On their way to the women's shelter were things I had bought specifically with him in mind. I discarded all textures and colors he enjoyed, as well as lingerie he had purchased for me. In one instance, I found myself with scissors in hand, destroying a beautiful silk nightgown he had given me just weeks before he left. I stuffed it into one of his dresser drawers for him to discover when he picked up the last of his things—proof, once again, that I must indeed be mean. I sold to a friend the lovely artificial Christmas tree we had purchased together our first year in our new home and acquired a new tree. There would be no reminders of the time I had lost to him.

The purging process remained ongoing—a continuous cycle of cleaning, sorting, shredding, and donating. I went drawer by drawer, item by item, eliminating every trace of the life he had left behind and the memories we had shared. I even emptied the refrigerator and pantry of staples, as most items had reached their expiration date. Each time I removed something, I experienced a brief respite from my pain. However, I was still unable to eat or sleep, as I continued my efforts to wrap my brain around the fact that my marriage was over and search for closure. I knew full well that without communication, I would receive no answers. How easy for him just to walk away. How cowardly to terminate, with no backward glance, the life we had shared, turning over to me all responsibility for cleaning up his mess. I was the one left to explain things to family and friends, to change memberships from family to individual, to cancel his subscription to the newspaper, and to handle all the other minute details required to end a marriage.

With every sweep through my house—every scrap of paper shredded, item donated, maintenance issue resolved—I gained greater clarity. I realized that the divorce would result in only a financial loss for him, while my loss would be emotional and far more painful. Each step left me drained but determined to regain normalcy and routine. I would continue to have fresh flowers and wine in my home, friends and family surrounding me, and a welcoming and inviting atmosphere for all who entered. Later, I would learn from therapy the phrase "mindless but meaningful," and the importance of focusing energy on even the smallest of accomplishments. But for now, I knew only that I was busy, felt productive, and relished even the most fleeting moments when I felt as if I had some control in my life.

Although I was scarcely capable of focusing, was unable to read a magazine article, and could not even consider a book, I was grateful for the many modern-day miracles that came my way each day. There were the lyrics of a song that inspired me. The mantras friends provided to aid in my survival. Each morning, a text reminding me to "find the good in today" would greet me. As I focused on that one little reminder, the beauty that remained all around me momentarily replaced the pain that persisted within. My older daughter shared a quote —"You have everything it takes, but it will take everything you have"—that I copied onto a large whiteboard and placed against my bathroom mirror. Each time I passed by, it helped to motivate me to keep going forward. It was anonymous and easy to remember, and fit my situation perfectly. So many times, I found myself internally repeating the words, which kept me inspired to accomplish whatever task was at hand.

There were cards that arrived in the mail, and the ever-present and always beloved tulips. With a change of perspective, I found myself viewing even my favorite flower differently. I watched them rise, bend, and stretch toward the light, searching for all the life that was available. They had a resilience and desire to thrive. Even when cut and without a food source, they continued to grow and reach for the sun—for hope. They would linger and hold on, despite the odds. Tightly closed when I first brought them into the house and placed them in a vase, tulips would open their petals to new life, new potential, a new adaptation—much as I knew I myself must learn to do.

I found myself working hard to restructure my thinking. Life as I had known it was over. Having never been one for television, I began watching *Downton Abbey* and the new show *Madam Secretary*, simply to connect with others who watched. Surprisingly, I found them quite entertaining and enjoyable as I began to heal and became caught up in both.

During the first holiday season, my loss felt crippling, my world empty, and tears rolled down my cheeks as I dug out cherished ornaments and set about celebrating on my own. However, I continued to embrace the love of family and friends. I hosted tree-trimming and cocktail parties at Christmas, as I had always done and which I greatly enjoyed. I purchased cards and wrote lengthy personal notes of thanks inside for service members. I even spent a long weekend in New York with Robbie that very first holiday season alone. I experienced moments of pure and unexpected joy as I watched snow fall on the tree in Rockefeller Center, viewed the Rockettes' holiday performance, and Christmas-shopped in the Big Apple. I made sure that Santa left presents for me under the tree and was brought to tears by the generosity of my children and Robbie, who offered piles of thoughtful and humorous gifts for me to open as well. He was not going to take my love of Christmas away from me. He had taken enough.

I purchased a new tablet, and because technology always made me feel awkward and inept, for too long I found myself using it only for email and online searches. I struggled repeatedly, until I finally reached out for help. I could conquer this. Calling first upon a high school–age neighbor, I gained some control over my new machine. Soon, however, there was a Windows 10 update and I was back to square one. I went to Amazon, ordered the *Dummies* version for seniors, and walked myself through the training. Amazingly, I gained the upper hand and was rewarded with a huge sense of accomplishment.

Instinctively, I became aware of a sense of the need for more options as I continued to experience the changes occurring in my world. Driven by something more powerful than I, I sought advice from the realtor who had assisted us in the purchase of our house. We had become friends, and she generously worked up a market analysis on my home and plugged me into a search engine of locally available properties in my price range. Concurrently, I connected with a realtor closer to my daughters who did the same thing. Still feeling powerless and frozen in place, I knew movement was required and options needed to be weighed. The home I had created was my only refuge and provided the motivation and soothing inspiration I desperately sought. Yet, given his totally unexpected change in behavior and commitment, I began to realize he might force me to leave. I was certainly not prepared for or ready to make an immediate move, but I did know that it was important that I have choices.

I had no income. While I had offered to return to teaching upon our arrival, I had been out of the profession for five years. I had no connections and no marketability, and I was sixty years old. I had retired to accompany him to this new location and was not eager to jump back into the workplace without careful consideration of what my options might be. Change was likely imminent, and I would not be in control of the timing of that change—regardless of how strong or how weak I might feel. I promised myself that while I might lose it all, I would not go down without a fight. Mechanically, I moved through the motions of searching for another place to live. Fortunately for me, I had a long-distance friend, Mary-Ann, who had just retired. She could offer support to me on speakerphone as I circled, zeroing in aimlessly on listings, while confused tears rolled down my cheeks.

I learned to present the facts and information of my life and my circumstances in terms others could understand. I explained that my husband had grown tired of married life and that he had walked away. His sudden change of heart surprised them, too. I accomplished the renegotiation of my cable and gas bills, regained control of my bank accounts, and adjusted and adhered to the budget that the forensic CPA who had represented me had created. I refinanced *my* home—a result of mediation—to secure a more comfortable payment.

As the process moved forward, I found myself guiltily enjoying two pleasures in my life. I smiled each time I bought a new throw pillow because I was acquiring something that I had always enjoyed and he had always scorned. Equally pleasurable was each lingerie purchase. I had always been a sucker for pajamas and panties, and, as he had enjoyed them on me, money had never been an issue for those items. My acquisitions now often came from the sale rack of overstock stores, rather than from the exclusive boutiques where I had shopped before. They now sometimes included synthetic fabrics, instead of exclusively silk. Still, I savored the knowledge that he would no longer delight in seeing me in such items. That pleasure belonged, once again, only to me. Ultimately, an oversize T-shirt I had purchased for my father to humor him through his rehab became one of my favorite sleeping choices.

Memory by memory, closet by closet, and room by room, I continued. Soon, I realized that my friendship garden needed to be purged as well. While I had always thought myself cautious in selecting those to have around me, my garden was long overdue for weeding. I had no strength or desire for betrayal or negativity. I required optimism and sincerity now more than ever. I needed to yank out and discard wilting specimens in the forefront. I needed to move some from the periphery to a place of better light and visibility, where they could flourish and grow.

I gave a few, which had languished from neglect, the proper attention, and those became some of the strongest and most beautiful treasures of all. My old friend Mary-Ann returned to my life in a more active role. We had graduated from the same college, taught at the same school, and kept in touch with letters and visits over the years as I'd found myself moving from state to state. When she learned of my situation, she made arrangements to fly from Chicago for a visit. Although she had family members who required her care and could stay only a week, she provided crucial support, inspiration, and strength, which continued and increased over time. The rekindling of old and the nurturing of fledgling relationships were some of the hidden benefits of this most painful process, as new connections developed into admired and trusted friends.

Each day—each moment—I struggled not just to replace old pillows and pictures with new, but also to replace my old life with a new, recognizable, and enhanced version of what I had come to know. My life had become similar in feeling to the hurricane-prone area in which I lived. I had been left to sweep away the debris and rebuild in the aftermath of the devastating storm and destruction of my marriage. I needed to resurrect what loss had devastated. I hoped one day I would reach a point where new was better than what I had known. A day when pain and grief would be left behind, and growth and healing would take their place.

As I continued to peel away layer after layer, I found myself changing and metamorphosing, moving toward my new normal. I didn't know where the road led or how I would realize when I had reached my destination. I was on the most difficult and unexpected journey of my life, without a compass or a map. I was unsure whether I would have the fortitude to continue moving forward—even with the support I was receiving. I did, however, know that I could never go back and was beginning to understand that it would not benefit me even if I could. I had no choice but to persevere, for I knew I could not give up.

CHAPTER FOUR

Just Because He Says It Doesn't Mean It's True

"The greatest act of faith some days is to simply get up
and face another day."

—AMY GATLIFF, *THE POWER TO NEVER GIVE UP*

O NE OF THE MOST URGENT AND DIFFICULT STEPS
in my grieving process was finding a qualified therapist
with whom I would feel comfortable and whose services, with
luck, health insurance would mostly cover. Although I had
sought professional advice throughout tumultuous or stressful
times during and after my first marriage and had even talked
with a therapist before my second marriage, in hopes of making it even more certain of success, I knew that this time it was
imperative that I find a "perfect fit." Yet people made to feel as
shameful as I are sometimes reluctant to initiate conversation
or question others regarding professional help of that sort.
Often, information on the Internet is outdated and unreliable.
There is always the emergency number on the back of one's
health insurance card, if all else fails. However, my pain felt
too intense, too immense, and too overwhelming to leave it up
to that kind of free-for-five-sessions number.

My insurance website offered a starting point where I

could search for family therapists in my area. I knew I wanted to speak only to a woman about my situation, so I immediately ruled out all male therapists. Experience was vital, so I next looked for someone with extensive years in the profession, someone in my own age range. Board certification was equally imperative, so I narrowed the field yet again. Location was also important, as I preferred not to have a long drive each way, especially at the beginning, when "fragile" didn't begin to describe my mental or emotional state. Grieving is a long process, especially in cases when there is no communication, clarification, or understanding of how a situation developed.

I made a list of several women I thought might be good candidates and cross-referenced them online. I searched for discrepancies in reviews, as well as client remarks, updates, and satisfaction ratings. It felt much like finding an attorney by watching accident commercials on television. If I had it to do again, I would pray for the strength to talk to trusted friends and get personal recommendations. I would ask for the courage to share the unspeakable anguish his words conveyed to me, and the horrific shame they caused me to feel. I would express the heartache and desolation I experienced in believing that I had destroyed my seemingly perfect life. I had shared those feelings only with Robbie and my daughters, and, without living in my location, they could suggest no professional support. Yet, finally, I found the name of the person I knew was right for me: a woman my age with a great deal of experience in such matters. Now, all I had to do was call her, set up the appointment, and then actually force myself to go.

While conducting the research took several days, making the phone call was even harder and took an equal amount of time. I finally summoned my courage and made the call, only to reach her voice mail. I later discovered it was often the case to initially reach only voice mail with family therapists who take their own calls and are routinely in session. When the return call came, from a very kind and patient receptionist, I discovered the therapist's next available appointment was three weeks away—another unsurprising event with a sought-after professional. But I was in despair. How could I survive until the available date? I would have to busy myself with routine chores, force myself to the fitness center, and rely heavily on supportive phone calls from family and friends.

On the morning of the appointment, I dressed and left hours earlier than necessary, thinking I would fool myself into making an outing of this experience. I would explore all the little shops and restaurants surrounding the office. I was unable to distract myself as long as I'd hoped to, and I arrived more than an hour ahead of schedule, nearly hyperventilating and on very shaky knees.

I parked and stepped out of the car. Walking through the door took all my strength. I was about to relate the humiliating story of what a terrible person I was and how I had destroyed a perfect marriage by being selfish and mean.

The receptionist, the kindest woman I may have ever met, warmly welcomed me into a cozy, homelike environment. She spoke to me in the soothing voice typically reserved for calming young children and frightened animals as she began to take down my personal information. Feeling a bit of confidence and offering a timid smile as I reached into my wallet for my insurance cards—I had a primary and a secondary provider—I received a knowing smile in return as she informed me that the doctor took no insurance. The fee was $200 per session.

That instant became one of the unforgettable moments of my ordeal. I had existed in a mostly vegetative state for the weeks following my husband's unexpected and unexplained departure. I knew that I could not work through this on my own. I had used every bit of strength and reserve I could muster to find a therapist and get myself to the appointment. I collapsed at the knowledge of an error in updated information and knew that at those prices, this doctor was not a realistic choice for my budget. Having plenty of time, I asked for a moment to think. I stepped outside and sat on the wraparound porch. Flowers were blooming and birds were chirping as I tried hard not to break down into tears. I texted my friend Robbie and, out of habit, my husband. They had always been my trusted advisors, and at this moment I felt in desperate need of help. I asked for their advice, already knowing that whatever their replies, I had to talk to this therapist, no matter the cost. Not surprisingly, both concurred: I did not have the strength to go forward another day on my own.

Having made the decision and feeling somewhat composed, I went back inside. I explained that I would like to keep the appointment after all. I would mail a check to the office immediately upon my return home; this office did not accept debit or credit cards. I was calmly assured that it was not a worry. Indeed, the receptionist would be looking for another fit for me, someone even closer to my home and who would take my insurance. True to her word, she did just that—even scheduling an appointment and putting me on a waiting list for an earlier appointment date if an opening were to become available. Everything was settled before the current session had begun. There *was* a reason I had arrived early.

Suddenly, it was time for the appointment. Taking a very deep breath and tightly gripping the banister, I climbed the flight of stairs to a second-floor parlor. A petite woman with a warm smile and welcoming demeanor shook my hand while introducing herself to me. She offered me a seat in a wing chair adjacent to hers, in front of a cozy fireplace. This room was a noticeably more comfortable temperature than what I had experienced at the attorney's, and I appreciated that. There was no fire, as the weather was still warm, but, given my trembling and shivering bunch of emotional nerves, I certainly could have absorbed the heat.

Crisscrossing my feet beneath me, fighting back tears, and continuing to focus on the fireplace, I began to tell my story as accurately and objectively as possible while the doctor typed away on her iPad, taking down every word. When I reached the part where we were in the car on the way to the lake, there was total silence as her fingers stopped flying across the keyboard. Moments passed, and, for the first time, from an objective professional, I heard the words "This is not about you. People with abandonment issues are not good communicators."

I continued to tell my story, hearing it again from start to finish and realizing that it all sounded unimaginable. Trying to regain a bit of dignity and inject a touch of humor after taking up far longer than the time allowed for the session, I asked this wonderful human being who might play my role in this made-for-TV drama. Giving me another warm smile and embracing me in a hug, the therapist pulled back, looked me in the eye, and responded, "A woman with the utmost dignity."

Relief washed over me after I had shared my story, and she sent me on my way. Once again alone, I faced the long journey home. While her words echoed in my mind and lessened some of the guilt that had been massed upon me, I was still confused and emotional. I still felt helpless and lost. I returned to an empty house, an empty life, and no sense of direction.

Fortunately, I did not remain in the abyss as long as I had anticipated. A cancellation occurred, and I could see the second therapist in a matter of days—and she was only fifteen minutes from my home. Feeling confident that long-term help had arrived, and that I would have the professional guidance and support I needed to begin to muddle through this nightmare, I made my way to her convenient but sterile office, anticipating rescue. Another deep breath, another retelling, another affirmation: "This is not about you, nor about dropping marbles into someone's jar." Then the words "You will find your way out of this with the right guidance from the right therapist."

"What? Why not you? *You* are right for me. I like *you*. I like how you listen. I need help. *Now!*" However, my insurance would not cover visits with this therapist. She worked with patients who experienced severe depression and saw them only to prescribe and administer drugs. I required none. Yet this was the second therapist who assured me that this was not my fault and that I was experiencing only situational depression. Did they not see that the depression encompassed every situation? How could I go home? How could I go on? I had never experienced such pain, nor felt so abandoned. I had so little strength. Collapsing, sobbing, with a dripping nose, I found myself once again wrapped in the arms of a professional and caring stranger who escorted me to my car. The therapist placed a paper with a name and number in my hand, and again I was told, "Get home safely." She assured me there was help available and reiterated that none of this was my fault.

Armed with yet another name, this time that of a man (which was not the ideal), and having little hope that the third time would be the charm, after regaining my composure, I made yet another appointment. When the day and the time arrived, the experience in the waiting room, which felt like the psychiatric ward portrayed in low-budget movies, told me this was not right. Overheard conversations centered on lifestyles of drug usage, abuse, and neglect. When I met the therapist, I

assured him this was a waste of time for both of us and explained my reasons. He concurred, and I was headed home yet
again, this time with no hug, no catharsis, and no name. I was
back to square one.

I compiled another list of possibilities, reviewing all of my
previous notes and cross-referencing them yet again with insurance information online. I was battle worn but much more
savvy. This time, I confirmed up front my circumstance and
my need to talk at length and work through situational depression, and established that the therapist was in-network with
both insurance carriers.

I got lucky. I received pre-approval for 150 sessions—from
both providers—so I could talk and talk and talk. I was in! Another bonus: the therapist was a woman. She answered her own
calls. She could see me the following week. She was close, and
because she had personally answered my call, I had spoken with
her to arrange a visit, and I had explained my situation and
previous appointments, I believed I had a connection with her.

Having found a therapist after eight long weeks, I was
more than ready to move forward in this journey of pain and
nothingness, and it seemed I might be starting down the road
to healing and recovery. I waited only moments in a quiet an-
teroom before the therapist herself escorted me into a homey
nook of an office. I told my story yet again: the trip to the lake,
the lack of communication, the accusations. I heard a new set
of words that, once again, offered hope that this was not all my
doing. "Just because he says it doesn't mean it's true."

While my children and friends had been assuring me of
the same since the beginning of my nightmare, hearing the
words from a professional who didn't need or want to love and
protect me catapulted me to a new level of determination and
strength. When we scheduled a second appointment, for two

weeks later, I was elated. Things couldn't be as dire as I had thought if I could go two weeks between sessions. At last, I felt as if I was taking charge and at least copiloting my journey to a better place.

CHAPTER FIVE

The Night the Lights Went On in Carolina

"Life isn't about waiting for the storm to pass.
It's about learning to dance in the rain."

—UNKNOWN

GRIEF IS NOT PRETTY. NOR IS THE DEPRESSION that hovers near the outside borders of the hole left in our heart at the loss of the one we love. The circumstances matter little. A broken heart can indeed be felt. Depression is a constant shadow and a sinister presence preying on the one who suffers—pushing, prodding, and presenting an undesirable yet appealing escape from the reality of the ache that does not cease. Living is a painful chore. Routine choices become impossible to make. Decisions are tabled; forward movement is paused. Each day feels like treading water in the deep end of a pool filled with quicksand. One is left attempting to survive minute by minute, looking forward to day's end and the peace of sleep—if it comes. Death ceases to be frightening and becomes preferable to the daily struggle of survival while one endures such raw emotional pain. While not willing, or wanting, to end our own life, one hopes that some outside circumstance or event will end it, thereby putting a stop to the agony.

Three months had dragged by, and he made his second trip back to the house to collect his belongings, including the furniture and other items I had gathered and deposited in the garage. He would be taking his vehicle as well, so there would be another person on hand. I still felt numb, but I was determined that, unlike with the first removal, I would remain present and perhaps even communicate with him. I would make myself be strong.

As I awaited his arrival, I anxiously sipped my coffee on the screened porch. When the doorbell rang, I went to the garage to raise the door. There he stood. The man I had known and loved for years now seemed a perfect stranger. There was no hug. There were no words. He made no eye contact. It was as if he were made of stone. With him was a man younger than our children. Instinctively, I surmised that perhaps this was the son of the lover he maintained he had never taken. After no introduction and a minimal exchange, the two began loading both vehicles with what they could stuff inside. In and out between the garage and the house, I hoped for a word, an opening, an opportunity for an explanation about why this was happening at all. There was no change in his cold and distant demeanor. There was no attempt at conversation. There was only the reality of the emptying garage and the comment "The bike wouldn't fit." The garage door was lowered as they pulled away. As I had requested, he left behind his house keys. I would not see him again.

Trembling and unable to fight the onslaught of tears, I stumbled back to the porch, texted Robbie, and opened the wine. It was already past noon, it was the weekend, and self-medication had become the survival norm. The return call was immediate, as I had expected, and while I blubbered and drank, my friend offered support and condolences. She reminded me that all of this was undeserved. She told me that I was strong. She assured me that there would be judgment coming down for him, either in this life or in the next. I was being called back from the cliff and continued to drink through the call, which lasted most of the afternoon.

Exhausted from the entire experience, I offered my final words to my friend when my sobbing ebbed at last: "I'm going to bed. I am not in danger of hurting myself or feeling at all suicidal, but if God were to take me, I would like to be gone, as I don't have the strength to work through this." I could sense her smile even through the telephone. Knowing me better than I sometimes knew myself, understanding my emotional fatigue after the day's events, and confident in my personal resolve to continue to move forward, she replied, "Sleep well, my friend. I love you."

Hanging up, I rinsed and recycled the wine bottle, washed the wineglass, prepared coffee for the morning, and set the alarm for eight. As life always does, even under the most painful of circumstances, it was reminding me of the mundane tasks that required attending to—such as the servicing of my car, scheduled for the following morning. Having never changed out of my pajamas that morning, I brushed my teeth, blew my nose, and wiped away the lingering tears. Instantly asleep, I awoke feeling refreshed and alert, although a bit late, as the car had to be in by nine.

I had never heard the alarm, and it was already past eight o'clock. I hurried into the kitchen to switch on the coffee and then to the shower. I held little hope of making the appointment on time. I dressed quickly and dried my hair. I grabbed my travel mug on the way out and pressed the button to raise the garage door. The first thing I noticed as I climbed into the car and backed out of the garage was that the rain had returned and the skies were quite dark. Indeed, I had an eerie, almost surreal feeling as I traveled the narrow and flooded plantation road heading toward the car dealership. My hands gripped the wheel, and my eyes remained focused straight ahead in an attempt to will the rain away and the windshield clear. The unnerving feeling remained as I approached the traffic light and could glance at the clock on the dash. I might make it on time after all—a modern-day miracle.

Clearing the intersection, I noticed that traffic was unusually light and was once again grateful for my good fortune. As I covered the last few miles and approached the dealership, the eerie sensation returned as I noted, even from the highway, that something just didn't seem right. When I turned onto the correct street, I saw that chains were blocking the entrance to the service department. That had never happened before. I drove past to the next entrance. That one was blocked as well. When I paused to make sense of what might be happening, the voices from the radio came into focus and I heard that it was 9:00 p.m.

How could that possibly be? I must have slept only briefly and had arrived at my appointment twelve hours in advance. That would explain the surreal quality of the drive. Mustering what limited strength and resolve I had after the day's earlier emotion, I gave myself a quick shake, opened the lid of the travel mug for coffee to sustain me, and headed back home as the rain began again in earnest.

Fortunately, because of the weather and the hour, there were few vehicles on the single-lane country road. The night was quite dark, and I reduced my speed to avoid contact with the wild boar and deer that lived along this stretch of asphalt. Again, focusing on the road ahead, I became aware of a truck coming my way on the opposite side, as well as a truck following close behind me. Simultaneously, I felt my right rear tire slip ever so slightly off the pavement and into standing water. There was no shoulder and little margin for error. Instantly, I muttered a dual offering to the heavens: "Please don't let me overcorrect! *I don't want to die!*" Gripping the wheel more tightly than ever and focusing on the headlights to my front and to my rear, I was incredulous when my prayer was answered. The car corrected, and I remained in control.

At that moment, I knew that, despite my tremendous hurt, my lack of resolve, and the pain I was facing—and would continue to face—I really did want to live. Divine and earthly intervention, support, and assistance would enable me to continue my forward struggle.

Upon my safe arrival home after that harrowing experience, I finished my mug of coffee. With a weak smile upon my face, I texted my daughter and my friend. I related the details of my experience and shared the total absurdity of having arrived for an appointment twelve hours ahead of schedule. They were concerned for my well-being, and both offered to drive to me immediately. I thanked each of them but declined. I crawled back into the bed for a much-needed and very restful night of sleep. When I returned to the dealership the following morning, I passed my neighbor's vacant car on the side of that very same road. While it was immediately obvious that it had collided with a deer, only later did I learn that the neighbor's infant son had required hospitalization for a concussion. Their experience saddened me and, once again, reminded me of my own good fortune.

After the car had been serviced, I headed to the therapist to share my amazing story and renewed determination to move ahead. However, once more, I was reduced to sobbing and felt at a loss for how to do more than just try to keep from drowning in my circumstances. I stood face-to-face with this woman as she looked deeply into my eyes and said to me, "You must find something that is mindless but meaningful to lift you above all this muck." She suggested I volunteer at a charity—find something of importance that would put me in the company of others but require only minimal interaction. Something that required no thought and would involve no emotional energy.

That is how I found myself sorting cans at a food bank each week, mindlessly focusing on preparing boxes of food that would certainly mean a great deal to the families who received them. Week after week, I spent Monday afternoons sorting. I chatted with a variety of other volunteers about their lives, and how they had been drawn to this specific philanthropic experience. We debated the most efficient way to sort the items that were always reappearing in front of us. I learned that if I continually supplied questions, they would be so busy providing answers that they would lose interest in questioning me. I discovered common friends with some and the common thread among us all: gratitude that we were not on the receiving end of the boxes we carefully packed. Sometimes I even brought a friend with me to help sort and pack. Each week, as I scrubbed off the dirt of the work and returned to my home, I was filled with a deep appreciation for all that I did have in my world. And finally, after much support, guidance, and time, the next chapter of my life presented itself.

CHAPTER SIX

❧

Rescued

"If you want to lift yourself up, lift up someone else."
—BOOKER T. WASHINGTON

*W*HAT WAS I THINKING? WILL I EVER KNOW? AS I struggled to climb the interminable ladder out of grief, I certainly didn't need or want a puppy. I was barely able to care for myself. How could I possibly care for a dog? Yet, fourteen months after my world was torn apart, an unexpected rescue occurred while I was visiting my daughter.

A young puppy had been taken from her mother at only five weeks old and turned in to the animal shelter. My daughter, certain that her mother would benefit from a dog in her life, had asked them to be on the hunt for what she called a "mini-Lab" for me. When this puppy appeared, the shelter director immediately phoned my daughter, and she happily offered to foster the pup, with a plan in mind. I was adamant that I did not want a pet and certainly was in no mental or emotional condition to take on a responsibility of that magnitude. I was only beginning to keep one foot in front of the other and get through each day. The last time I had brought home a puppy had been during my first divorce. At that time, after years of hearing from my younger daughter how desperately she wanted a dog, I surprised her with it when a friend's dog had a litter. Now, as then, I knew little about the requirements and responsibilities of raising a dog, and this time there would be no daughters to help share the burden of responsibility. However, during my weekend visit, the campaign to wear me down was on. My daughter made suggestions about how much company a pet would provide: "You won't be alone anymore." She placed the puppy in my lap continuously: "See, she already likes you." She put forth ideas regarding the fun we would surely have together: "You can take her to the beach." I thought my resolve was strong, but as we played with the puppy and brainstormed names, I realized that this young animal, only six weeks of age, would somehow be making the trip home with me when I left.

Since the shelter had accepted the pup as their charge, the obligation for all of her initial vaccines and spaying was part of the contract with the agency. The pup had only her first round of shots, and until she had had them all, she was not to leave the vicinity. Because of my daughter's connection and support, the shelter director would allow me to leave town with the dog in tow. However, I had to promise to return her to them routinely when shots and spaying were due. I gave my word and purchased a small crate, and we headed for home. She was a calm and happy traveler from the start, although these recurring trips were suddenly longer in duration as frequent "potty" stops were required.

Though the puppy was a mere ball of creamy butterscotch–colored fluff, I marveled at her curiosity, determination, and zest for life. Because of the tenacity (and perhaps a mean streak) she seemed to possess, I named her Lucifer. She quickly began responding to the shortened and more loving version of her name: Lucy.

In the early days Lucy and I spent together, her crate stayed by the front door, as we traveled back and forth so often. She slept through the night easily and instantly. Accidents were rare. On one of our early and frequent potty trips to the backyard, it began to rain, and Lucy immediately headed to the door. I knew an accident would result if we went inside without her first doing her "business," so I placed her back in the yard to accomplish our goal. I stayed with her and insisted, "You have to go potty, and I am going to win." Lucy looked at me with a seemingly knowing grin and raced around the yard in circles until a torrential rain forced me to pick her up and take her inside—still without success. The quiet life was over; she was no longer concerned about storms or getting wet. It was readily evident that Lucy was in charge.

My leisurely retirement mornings of sleeping in were gone. While Lucy would quiet temporarily if I reminded her, "It's still dark," and waited patiently as I brushed my teeth and pulled on my clothes, she stirred with the first slivers of light passing through the shutters and eagerly anticipated the start of her day. As I unlatched her crate, my happy little charge seemed to dance across the floor in excitement as she headed for the door and the breakfast that would follow. Her enthusiasm for life and all that it might hold made me aware there were still many simple pleasures to enjoy, despite the pain I continued to feel.

When Lucy came in, the indoor plants went out. Intrigued by the smell, texture and availability of all plants, she happily set about gnawing and digging at every available species. My backyard, which had been lush and magazine-perfect before her arrival, was immediately altered and under constant attack as a result of her inquisitive nature. My efforts to deter her interest by spraying the plants with the hot sauce a friend suggested did not stop Lucy. It did affect the plants, however, as they burned and wilted. Fortunately, indoor plants could be removed, providing a safer and less stressful environment for dog and owner. I gave those plants away, and somehow, following their departure, I experienced another sense of discarding what had once seemed so important, and yet another restructuring of priorities.

Still, Lucy found she could chew inconspicuously by crawling under beds and furniture and tearing at hidden mesh. Once I discovered her secret and removed the fiber, she turned to the rug under the kitchen table and socks left momentarily unattended. When I provided a variety of chew toys, she happily redirected her attention. Lucy soon grew to be intrigued by her reflection in the refrigerator or full-length mirror and running circles around the open downstairs living space, where she was allowed free (but supervised) rein. Just keeping her safe and occupied seemed to fill up every minute.

Lucy quickly learned to identify and respond to the sound of the peanut butter jar and the yogurt container opening—two of her favorite treats. She waited patiently by the freezer door to stealthily remove an errant ice cube dropped from the ice maker. She would immediately take it to the rug to happily chew, before she returned, in hopes of finding more. She understood the words "power nap" and readily curled up on her bed so dog and owner could reenergize. Refreshed and stretching afterward, Lucy would happily return to her outside world to chase whatever she might find.

I was still avoiding contact with people in the neighborhood as much as possible, so at first we neglected walks. However, my neighbor, who owned two dogs of his own, repeatedly reminded me that Lucy needed to be on a leash and learn to walk. With his continued reassurance, we took on a new adventure. Having witnessed so many neighbors with their bags to clean up after their pets, I thought I could likely handle this type of outing. After all, I held an advanced degree and had thirty years of teaching and parenting experience. It wasn't as easy as it looked, and my ineptitude quickly surfaced. I somehow got the bag tangled, and the waste fell from the bag to the sidewalk with a distinctive *plop*. I took Lucy home and returned with another bag, paper towels, and a large bucket of water to clean up the mess. Again, I wondered, *What was I thinking?* But at least my humility remained intact.

When I noticed spaghetti-length worms in her stool, I located a vet close by and treatment began. It seems we had found our vet just in time. At the recheck for worms, Lucy was found to have ear mites as well, and more medication was required. This time, it was ear drops, and she didn't seem to think they were at all acceptable. At a time when I was trying to bond with my new puppy, she would avoid me at any cost, rather than have drops repeatedly applied to her ears. Setbacks aside, I was expanding my network.

I had not expected to adopt a puppy and had given little thought to the breed or the characteristics of the breed. Terms like "high energy," "intelligent," "loving," and "playful" seemed to apply to all young pups eager to explore their world. As a beagle-Lab mix, not only did Lucy possess boundless energy, but she also picked up on high-energy signals from her emotionally unsettled and frustrated owner. The combination of the two often made our coexistence a visible struggle. She was a hunter, digger, and retriever. She was proud to present each new treasure she discovered and captured, from lizards and entire plants with roots intact to rats and snakes. Most times, my enthusiasm did not come close to matching her excitement, and I often questioned my ability to maintain this pace.

Lucy provided, and perhaps expected in return, unconditional and selfless love. She opened my heart. She offered support in my fledgling efforts to move beyond heartache, and, as her owner, I was required to step outside my comfort zone and consider more than my own needs. Lucy needed playtime, sunshine, and lots of opportunities to go outdoors. She demanded training and attention, consistency and patience, and a great deal of time. Food and supplies required trips to the pet store, where I soon realized just how overwhelmed I was with a dog. Workers there consistently and hurriedly approached us upon our arrival. They wore worried looks on their faces and would ask how they might assist us (meaning me). Lucy happily accepted and came to expect the attention bestowed upon her at each visit. I just wanted to go home.

But gradually I began to put Lucy's needs first. I mastered scooping poop into little plastic bags. I sat on the floor with her, rather than on the furniture, and I placed cozy dog beds on the floor of every room where we spent time together. I felt my heart expanding and joy beginning to sneak in. I learned about appropriate chew toys and healthy food and snacks. I dedicated my Saturdays to her. Between long weekends of travel for her puppy round of shots, we were at puppy play programs at the Humane Society. I enrolled her in puppy training, where I was the least competent of any of the other dog owners. I took her for socializing at Lowes and Target, where her little feet fell through the openings of the shopping baskets as we attempted to acquire confidence while she encountered loud noises, strangers, and crowds. Of course, if I were going to teach Lucy to be fearless, I knew I must once again endeavor to be fearless myself. We learned to navigate the rules of local dog parks, and encounters with other dog owners in those settings. I purchased what I was told were the appropriate and approved collars, harnesses, and car restraints available in today's pet-friendly market.

I soon discovered that having a dog was as complicated as having a baby. I learned that, like babies, people respond to puppies, and "parents" want to do right by them. Because I was retired, I had made a full commitment of time and energy to my new charge. Each time I learned of a recommended training program or puppy socializing class, I registered Lucy and dedicated my time to it. The entire puppy adventure overwhelmed me, but I was assured that I would soon find and assimilate into groups of friends with dogs. I was doubtful that there would ever be light at the end of this tunnel, but I was unable to do anything less than forge ahead. I had survived the unexpected end of my marriage; surely I could manage Lucy.

I caught myself talking to her as I had talked to my daughters and students and marveled at how quickly her vocabulary grew. As in human relationships, I sometimes missed the mark for how best to handle her current needs and situation. We made modifications along the way and acquired extra support or alternate training whenever necessary. Trial and error raised my awareness of what Lucy required at any given moment to benefit each of us and to ensure that I could live up to the commitment of dog ownership. Each time I failed and required outside help, my world expanded and I developed new connections and friendships. With hard work and great determination, I was finally rewarded for my efforts with a reasonably well-behaved and companionable young dog.

Lucy's love of the outdoors and the sunshine on her face paralleled my own. When unable to be outside in direct sunlight, she would lie on the stairs, where the sun streaming through the windows would fall directly upon her. However, as I grew more willing to venture out, we spent much time outdoors, exploring the neighborhood, to the benefit of both of us. She forced me to move beyond my grief and solitude, and I soon knew the names of all the dogs and their owners we encountered on our frequent and lengthy walks. Long walks also provided me with time to reflect and think things through in an effort to formulate plans for moving ahead in my life. My world was indeed growing.

As Lucy and I continued meeting and interacting with people from all over the neighborhood, I expanded beyond the drinking buddies I had shared with my spouse and began enjoying a comfortable sense of belonging and ownership I had not experienced before. I met an inspiring elderly neighbor who still lived independently, engaged in meaningful conversation, delighted in making and sharing her traditional pierogi, and still worked outside in her yard on a daily basis. At the age of ninety-three, Mary became a role model for how I wanted to live when I reached her age. Lucy and I walked by her house several times each day, and I found myself looking forward to seeing her each time we passed.

None of these new friends seemed to care or to ask about my relationship with anyone apart from my dog. Before long, I found myself looking forward to these interactions with others and the tips and guidance they provided. Amazingly, Lucy was responsible for the development of one of my most treasured new friendships. A happy, chance meeting occurred on one of our walks, as we spied an unknown neighbor with a stunningly beautiful young pup tangled at the end of a long leash. As I stopped to offer help, we introduced ourselves and our pets. While Lucy sniffed and made Stella's acquaintance, Monika and I chatted briefly. As Stella and Lucy grew into the best of puppy friends, Monika and I developed a deepening friendship, trust, and respect for each other. Now, playdates between Lucy and Stella have become as eagerly anticipated by the owners as by the dogs themselves as we share conversation and camaraderie while the animals frolic happily in the backyard.

More than three years have passed since Lucy entered my life. We have both grown calmer and accustomed to each other, despite setbacks and frustrations. Retraining was sometimes necessary. Boarding arrangements were adjusted and playgroups rethought. I remain concerned that I will not have the energy Lucy will continue to require. Yet I have discovered there are many unexpected ways in which we can empower ourselves, and that raising a puppy is one of them. I found that by rising to my best, I allowed Lucy to be her best. I discovered that time spent training Lucy afforded me time for retraining myself to enjoy all that life offers. I marveled at the fact that watching her sleeping peacefully on her bed in front of the fire provided me with as much peace and tranquility as a day spent on the beach. I began to listen for the tiny yelps she would emit as she slept, and wondered what part of our day she was remembering in her dreams. I came to realize that Lucy was my very own service dog, who could calm me merely with her quiet breathing. And each time I encountered the catchy phrase "Who rescued who?" I smiled and offered a quiet prayer of thanks, because I know: Lucy rescued me.

At a time when it seemed like my life was over, Lucy gently led me to discover that it had in fact just begun. She selflessly and unknowingly afforded me the strength and healing that I so desperately required. I have no doubt that while I might have eventually made it to the place where I was meant to be, I would not have made it as quickly or as well without Lucy by my side. She provided a sense of peace and joy in my life that had been lost. As we share quiet moments of contentment over coffee and a bone on the porch, watching birds and lizards, or with wine and a bone in front of the fire, my heart never fails to explode with gratitude and love.

CHAPTER SEVEN

⟨⟩

The Hits Just Keep On Coming

"Sometimes you have to get knocked down lower than you've
ever been to stand up taller than you ever were."
—UNKNOWN

*P*EOPLE WILL TELL YOU THAT TIME HEALS. I
quickly discovered that time does not heal—it merely
passes. Healing does need time, but it also requires hard work,
probing questions, grieving, support, and determination. The
grieving process also demands more effort and includes more
setbacks than I had ever imagined. Even with therapy and an
improved sense of strength, I often felt as if I was losing my
sanity. I found myself crying over the gentle kindnesses others
showed me. The moment my friend who lived next door
walked over to ask, "How are you doing?" The time the handy-
man preferred by all in the neighborhood approached me one
day when I was walking Lucy and said, "I heard about what
happened. Anything you need, just give me a call." I believed
that what we put out to the world comes back to us.

Each day I was filled with gratitude for having inherited
my father's optimism and resiliency. I had been trying to maintain the positive, and much was returned to me. Still, I was also

unable to hide my vulnerability, and betrayal and loss appeared to be the outcome. I often felt confused, helpless, and alone.

Although I was fortunate to have the unwavering backing of trusted longtime friends, I had thought I could rely on those nearby who had sworn allegiance. However, that was not to be. Several who had pledged their loyalty and vowed lifelong friendship and support suddenly turned their backs on me, just as he had done. There was no explanation for the change, no concern for broken promises, no thought about the impact that their additional, unexpected abandonment had on me when I was already struggling to adjust to life in an unexpectedly altered way and was in such a fragile state. I was suddenly without the support upon which I had so desperately depended. Many just put me out of their minds. I felt as if I had become one of the group referred to as the walking wounded. My wounds, however, could not be seen, so they were easy to ignore. I understood the key to healing was not just seeking, but following, professional advice. I knew I had to find the strength to be less reactive and more proactive. I had to move forward with my life.

Down and up I went, struggling to regain my footing, hoping to find my equilibrium. I remained unable to find the resolution I so desperately sought in my efforts to reclaim normalcy after the shock of his leaving, followed by an absence of any type of communication from him. I had found a therapist. I was even working a bit in my profession, supervising student teachers at a local college. I had investigated the opportunity nearly two years before, when I had serendipitously met a woman at the fitness center wearing a sweatshirt from one of the local schools. I had struck up a conversation with her. Like I was, she was a relocated and retired teacher. She was working part-time at the college, supervising student teachers. We agreed to meet for lunch at a later date to discuss details as our fitness class was about to begin. At lunch, she outlined the expectations of the position she held and provided insight into the rewards and the drawbacks of working with students. She provided the contacts for the three colleges in our area and wished me the best. I quickly sent my résumé to all three schools but was told there were currently no opportunities. When I got the call inquiring about my continued interest, it was poorly timed. Jim had been gone less than a year, and I was still confused by my new situation. However, I was well educated, vastly experienced, and looking for a diversion. Those first students probably did not get my best. I had received little training or guidance and was still finding it difficult to focus. Still, even at less than my personal best, I believed I provided them with the professional leadership and caring insights I attained over my thirty-year career. Yet the hits just kept on coming. Setback after setback occurred, and I again questioned my ability to endure.

When my daughters were toddlers, they had an inflatable clown that was child-size and weighted at the bottom. They would giggle with delight each time they punched him down and he returned to stand tall in front of them, awaiting the next blow. I felt as if my life were becoming that of the clown. Small but immediate challenges began to pop up. The outdoor blind snapped; the kitchen light that had just been working suddenly blew out; the garage door opener failed. I was tested further when the furnace gave out on the coldest of days, the main water valve to the house broke off, and I found myself balanced precariously, straddling a ladder and a railing as I tried to replace the bulbs in an outdoor light that had suddenly shattered in my hands. Problems began dramatically increasing in frequency and escalating in intensity as the weeks and months continued to pass. At least it seemed that way to me.

When I learned my next-door neighbors were moving, I experienced a major blow. I had removed myself from Facebook, so I had seen no posts that would have alerted me to the change. I realized that something was amiss only when I noticed strangers touring their house one day. When I spoke with my neighbor and learned the news, I knew another unexpected and painful loss was about to occur. This family had reached out in friendship from the moment we had met. All three had provided sincere and constant support to me when I was left alone. I would miss them greatly, and I was despondent.

My daughter had done all the research and arranged for delivery of a much-needed new vehicle. When I arrived to pick it up and sign the paperwork, the sales rep had sold the car to someone else. I suggested that the situation sounded like a classic example of a bait and switch. The general manager suggested that I would be happier with another dealership that could locate and service my new vehicle. Fortunately, I identified an alternative, though it was much farther from my home. Less than a week after I received my new vehicle, a tow truck backed into my car as I waited in the parking lot to meet a friend for lunch.

There was also the small patio that had been created in my backyard the weekend before the fateful trip. It had looked perfect upon completion, but then heavy rains had washed it out and it had already been redone three times. It remained barely usable and not at all what I had envisioned as I strove to maintain the home's appearance. If it happened that I would need to sell at a future date, the patio would surely have to be rebuilt. But for now, I could give it no further thought.

Finally, as expected, my husband's brother died several months after the trip to the lake. While I had always admired and respected him, no one in the family had communicated with me since our trip to the lake, so I had not had the opportunity to say goodbye. I received only a perfunctory text from my husband telling me that his brother was gone. I lost the connection with his brother's wife as she, too, disentangled herself from a family that had little use for her now that her husband was deceased. I lost my relationship with his children and grandchildren, whom I had worked so hard to blend into a loving and compassionate unit.

I needed to refinance my home in my own name, and when it was time, I discovered that conventional loans were unobtainable without a six-month history of spousal support. I had only two months. I was walking Lucy one day, and when we stopped to play with Stella, her best puppy friend, a neighbor's dog got loose and attacked—not one of the dogs, but me. I was left with a deep wound, a lasting scar, and a dog not quite as socially confident. Lucy required one-on-one training at the cost of $100 per hour, which was certainly not in my budget. I hoped to avoid stitches and the series of shots I would require if the dog had rabies.

My father had heart valve replacement surgery. My sister-in-law, who we all thought had successfully battled breast cancer and who had been in remission for years, was suddenly confronting the disease once again. While she remained stoic and optimistic about the recurrence, my brother was clearly worried, and I feared for what his life would become if he were to lose her. My father and brother both resided in distant states and deserved my attention. So, once again, I prepared and froze food for all, then embarked on the thirteen-hour trip to provide support. I was relieved to see my father meet me in the drive with the use of a walker, and I savored the lovely three-day visit with him and his wife.

My time with my brother and sister-in-law was not as pleasurable. While my sister-in-law was fatigued but in good spirits, my brother was less than welcoming. His initial complaint against me was that I had failed to arrive at the exact time he wished—even though I had determined my arrival time in advance with his wife. Respectful of the need of privacy for all, and wishing not to intrude on their lives, I stayed at a hotel, rather than in their home. My choice irritated him even further. I believed his anger resulted from his concern for his wife, and was determined to remain upbeat and helpful. That, it appeared, was the problem. He told me that I was "too nice" and making his wife "think about her condition."

I wondered, *Would his wife not know about her condition if she were treated unkindly?*

Later, he told me to terminate all communication until I received word from him that I could once again be a part of their lives.

I remained confident that, as siblings, we would resolve the issue over time and heal this wound. But for now, I was forced to deal with yet another painful and unexpected loss.

I departed ahead of schedule and texted my therapist to arrange an immediate meeting upon my return. I was confused about how I could possibly be "too nice" and "too mean" at the same time. As we sat in her office a few days later, she explained to me that people, in addition to substances, could prove toxic to our well-being. I clearly understood her message and, for the time being, knew that I would distance myself from my brother, as well as my husband.

I reached a significant turning point in my journey when I received word from my daughter of an unexpected and potentially life-threatening health scare she was facing. She had provided so much daily support to me throughout this ordeal; she deserved the same loving attention and backing from me as she confronted this unexpected obstacle. It was time I leave behind the role of victim to resume the role of mother. I was much more comfortable with and successful in that position, and, at that moment, I was reminded of my priorities: there was nothing more important to me than my daughters.

I phoned my attorney and informed her that I had no strength left to fight the marital battle. The divorce would have to go on without me. I was unsure of the logistics that statement would entail, but I would no longer be available to address insignificant arguments or unwavering and unreasonable offers. When real movement occurred, I could be notified and would do whatever was required. Until that time, I would trust her to act in my best interest, and I would focus on what really mattered in my life.

As my father continued to heal, complications and side effects with surgery and medications set in. His wife, Audrey, contracted bacterial meningitis. I was arranging for my rotation among family members to provide care and support for the two of them, when my father died unexpectedly. I was devastated that I had missed seeing him before his death, and I flew immediately to their home to help with arrangements and support his widow. I helped her to select songs for the funeral Mass, as well as the flowers that would be on display. We ordered red roses from Blooms by Sandy—the same local florist my father had patronized by purchasing countless red roses for his wife to honor each of their special occasions.

I was also the person assigned to the job of assisting Audrey in sorting through his belongings. We patiently collected prescription drugs and medical equipment to be properly discarded or returned. Others teamed up to mow the lawn, plant flowers in outdoor beds, and clean each room from top to bottom—all tasks that had been neglected during his illness and recovery. I sat with her to sort through the closets and the clothing that had belonged to him. We found unopened packages of socks, T-shirts, and underwear and put them into a pile to donate, along with dozens of pairs of shoes. The coat closet was cleared, and coats that had been his were offered to his son and grandsons. Any that were unwanted were also added to the pile to donate.

Once again, I found myself purging the belongings of a man I had deeply loved. Eliminating reminders of my husband had felt very personal and very real. I had recognized every item, photo, letter, and piece of jewelry, each of which symbolized a special and personal memory of the nearly fifteen years we had shared, and reminded me of that unexpected loss.

Going through my father's belongings was an equally emotional but very different experience. There had been a great deal of geographic distance between us, as we had both relocated to share our lives with our new spouses. Phone calls had been frequent and visits routine, but the miles between us had compromised our day-to-day connection.

As I handled each of my father's belongings, I was overcome with a different sense of loss. Except for the bathrobe I had sewn for him for Christmas many years before, I had few recollections of the occasions on which he had worn these clothes, or the intimate details of the new life he had made with the woman seated beside me. As with my husband's, my father's departure was unexpected and created a huge void in my heart where love had once dwelled. However, unlike my husband's love, my father's love was ever present, truly unwavering, and impossible to replace.

As I checked his pockets and sifted through his belongings, I experienced a real sense of the love he had felt for this woman sitting beside me. I extracted dozens of suits from his closet. Each suit was carefully hung with several coordinating dress shirts beside it. Pocket squares, belts, and cuff links were there as well. There was a white dinner jacket and a formal tuxedo. There were matching shoes, with a spit-polished shine, for each of his outfits. I remembered my father's having had only one suit and perhaps three pairs of shoes during my childhood. When I asked Audrey about the dramatic change, she replied, "Your father liked going out and being with people. He enjoyed looking nice."

I learned that his wife and her children had purchased most of these clothes as gifts to help him attain that goal. To me, what I was looking at was the closet of a man who proudly escorted his wife, whom he loved dearly, on his arm whenever they stepped out to enjoy a social occasion. There would be people in need all around town wearing my father's happy memories.

As a military veteran, my father would be buried in Arlington National Cemetery. Therefore, I had to gather strength both for services in his town of residence and for a trip to Arlington four months later. At the viewing and service, I began to fixate on the fact that I had been unable to say goodbye to my father before he died, and continually went over the details of our last telephone conversation, the day of his death. I always ended conversations with those I cared for by saying, "I love you." However, that day, there was chaos on his end, as he was confined in a hospital room and ordered to rehab. His unintelligible ramblings to "get me out of here; I will not stay" left me helpless to calm him or understand his needs. When his wife and her daughter arrived, I asked that he put Audrey on the line as we struggled to soothe his fears and speak with doctors. In the chaos, the phone was passed off without my telling him, "Goodbye, Dad. I love you."

Fortunately for me, Robbie had flown in to provide added support, as had my friend Mary-Ann, who drove down from Chicago. My daughters were there as well. Surrounded by family and friends who lifted me both emotionally and physically, I said goodbye to my remaining parent. It was not until the local American Legion unit fired the traditional rifle rounds to honor his passing that I knew he was indeed gone.

The service in Arlington, as expected, was even more emotional and challenging. Having lived on army bases, I was aware of the protocol and the tradition of the military. I knew how moving the bugle playing taps at the end of the day could be even when one was not mourning a loss. This would be a real test of my emotional strength and well-being.

When the time for the final burial arrived, I embarked once again on a difficult journey. Lucy and I had grown accustomed to the travel between South Carolina and Virginia. However, the distance from Indiana to Virginia was far more daunting, especially for an elderly widow in the early stages of grieving. Audrey's children made plans for her to fly directly to Washington, DC, where her daughter and son-in-law would pick her up. It would be a long and arduous trip for her, so I made hotel reservations for the two of us close to Arlington. We left our respective homes to travel toward our final destination on the appointed day. I dropped Lucy off with my daughter in Richmond. The next day, I headed farther north to check in to the hotel and confirm final arrangements.

When Audrey arrived with her daughter, we left the hotel for a bit of a distraction. Her grandson and great-grandchildren had also arrived, in a show of support, and we wanted to spend time with family over dinner, during which we experienced a range of emotions. The following day, we would take full advantage of the museums as we wheeled Audrey through the buildings of the Smithsonian, which she had not visited in years. The cold and blustery winds made being indoors extra appealing—especially for me, having left summer weather and flip-flops just days before. As more family arrived, we again shared a meal that evening, before retiring to bed early to prepare for the day ahead. The weather for the day of burial forecast a cold drizzle—typical early-October weather in our nation's capital. We had all prepared for such conditions, but the morning dawned sunny and warm—a day my father would have noticed and appreciated.

On average, thirty burials per day occur at Arlington National Cemetery. The precise coordination of handling that many events and moving that many people made me conjure images of an air traffic control center at a major airport. I drove from the hotel to the cemetery, with Audrey and her granddaughter as my passengers. We had a handicapped tag because of Audrey's frail health and were escorted immediately to a reserved space in front of the main building. We checked in, were directed to the room that had been assigned to our family, and awaited the arrival of the burial coordinator who would guide us through the day. I would have no friends who appeared this time, like superheroes, to offer much-needed soothing.

Family continued to trickle in, and I was especially relieved to see and embrace my daughters upon their arrival. When our burial coordinator entered the room, he appeared somewhat agitated and demanded, "Who owns the vehicle with the South Carolina plates that is parked in the handicapped loading zone?" That, of course, was me. A difficult experience was having an auspicious start. The vehicle was instantly moved, and we awaited further instructions about how the event would progress. The immediate family was called out to speak with clergy and provide insight for final words.

The solemn tradition and finely orchestrated protocol of a military funeral is much like that of royalty. In the United States, every soldier has the option of burial in this hallowed place. Enlisted personnel are treated with the same deference as the President. I drove the lead vehicle in the procession, as I was carrying the First Lady—the widow of the soldier about to be put to rest. Before we had even had a chance for our full entourage to assemble behind us, everything ahead stopped and the coordinator once again approached my vehicle. I lowered my window and wondered what I could possibly have done wrong now.

"Ma'am," he admonished, in a much softer tone than the one he had used with me previously, "I know you're from South Carolina. However, we're in Virginia, and even in Arlington we drive a bit faster than you're going. Please keep less than a car length between you and the vehicle you're following." Not wanting to throw a wrench into such a meticulously planned event, I proceeded on my way, making sure to honor his request. I understood that many families were experiencing the same sense of loss as I was and were waiting anxiously to lay their loved ones to rest.

We followed the hearse to the previously determined midpoint. All who attended stopped, stepped out of vehicles, and watched with pride and sadness as precisely groomed soldiers transferred the casket to a horse-drawn caisson. Audrey and I stood entwined and squeezing each other tightly. We worked to control our tears and hold each other upright, just as we had done at the memorial service four months earlier.

When that portion of the ceremony was complete, the procession solemnly made its way through the most precisely maintained acreage in the city of Arlington. At the gravesite, comforting words were spoken, taps played, the flag presented, and rounds fired. The shell casings were collected and presented to the grieving widow, and the family was escorted out—as they had been escorted in—by their personally appointed burial coordinator.

After the service and the family gathering that followed, we drove back to our hotel. We changed into pajamas, welcomed my daughter, and shared a relaxing and pleasant evening together, reminiscing over a bottle of wine and room service. My daughter returned home that night, and the next morning, after breakfast, Audrey's daughter took her to the airport while I began the drive back to my home. The man we had both loved had been officially laid to rest.

I WAS WALKING Lucy one Sunday morning the following September, nearly two years after Jim left, when I ran into a neighbor and stopped to chat. I anticipated where the conversation, and the neighbor, would head. I hoped this time it would be different.

Every Sunday, this woman, her husband, and another neighborhood friend and her husband went for brunch at the clubhouse nearby. I knew this was their routine and their time, and I always tried to ignore the emptiness I felt when they failed to invite me. Today, somehow, I was unable to shake those feelings of loneliness and pain. I wasn't asking to be a regular part of their group, but could I not be included on occasion? I thought they understood how much it would mean to me. After all, they knew the details of my situation. I did not want to disrupt, did not want to steal one of their men—I wanted only an hour of friendship and an escape from the emptiness of my days. Each week that I saw them, I played my practiced conversational loop in my mind. I would pretend to be surprised by their invitation to include me. I would politely decline but allow myself to be convinced to accept and accompany them just this once. I would thank them for allowing me to join them and wish them a relaxing day.

I fought back the tears as my neighbor told me once again that she and the others were heading to brunch. My dear pup, Lucy, immediately alert to a variation in body language and sensing my emotional change, led me quickly back to the security of my home. When the garage door closed behind us and we were safely inside, my tears fell. I announced to my pup, as there was no one else there to listen or to care, that it seemed to be time to leave this place and move on.

I had moved so often in my life that I knew how to take control of a relocation. I immediately googled storage units. I contacted my realtors in both states to reactivate my search engines for homes in my price range. I was still working only part-time at the college, so leaving a job would play no part in my decision. I alerted my financial advisor that change was on the horizon and explained that we would need to have an immediate discussion about monies, as I would likely need funding for a new home.

I had lined up my professional network and felt determined to move forward—and out. I next turned to my personal network and received one consistent bit of insight from all three individuals.

I made my first call to Mary-Ann, who listened patiently to the recounting of my experience. She confirmed my feelings and validated my decision with her immediate retort, "I never really saw you settling there forever."

The response from Robbie was a bit different, as she sympathetically suggested, "We are here to offer our continued and total support to you in whatever you choose to do. Whether you stay where you are or choose to move will likely be the hardest decision you will ever make. You will know the right time to make that decision. However, today is perhaps not the right time. Because you have been hurt by a casual acquaintance, you might not be thinking clearly or reacting sensibly."

Audrey was the most direct in her assessment of the situation and her interpretation of how best to handle it. "Get yourself some real friends outside the neighborhood. Get involved with other people. Get busy, get out, and refocus your life on *you*. If you still want to leave, we're here to back you. You will know when the time is right, but for right now, take a bit more time."

So I was again propelled ahead and began another chapter in my efforts to discover a new normal for myself as I determined to follow their sage advice. Through all of these experiences, I knew I needed resilience and determination, but I despaired of ever finding either. However, little by little, the solutions to these problems appeared, and my improving circumstances opened windows onto new insights as I determined to explore potential opportunities for a new life right where I was, before I contemplated uprooting myself yet again.

EIGHT MONTHS AFTER Jim left me, I had rallied the strength required to return to an exercise class at the fitness center. Understandably, women I had spent hours with each week were surprised and happy to see me again. I pulled aside those I had been closest to and briefly updated them on what had transpired over the missing months. A big step. But even bigger was the new woman, Judy, who introduced herself. She was from Boston and recently retired. She and her husband had purchased a condo in the neighborhood, thinking they would move south when they had both retired. While her husband was still working and remained in Boston, she had decided to stay in South Carolina on her own for the entire winter. She wanted to get a real feel for how they might like it if they settled here permanently.

After class, the two of us chatted and went for coffee and biscotti. We experienced an immediate connection over a long and intimate conversation. I was filled with joy to have met a woman my age who was open, frank, and available during the days. We shared frequent workouts, a dining and painting outing, and a spontaneous alfresco dinner on my porch. Then spring arrived and Judy was gone. She returned home, and I was again left alone.

Nevertheless, the memories and positive feelings from my experiences with her were enough to nudge me in the direction of venturing out to new activities and meeting new people. I was hopeful that I would find another woman to befriend, another opportunity to step outside my box. I had to dig deep and go back and try again. I knew there were people in existence as eager as I was to explore new activities and new friendships. I must reach out and find them.

I returned to my laptop and the Internet. If "trying times are for trying new things," I needed to discover something new. I needed to broaden my support system. I found a local book club, which would be meeting that Thursday. I ordered Erik Larson's *Dead Wake: The Last Crossing of the Lusitania* and read it on my Kindle, anxiously anticipating the gathering. It was not easy to walk into that group, but all were welcoming and supportive, and we had an animated and insightful discussion about the book. I was intrigued by the depth of research the members had done, not only on the *Lusitania*'s history but also on the author's background—including details of his research process. I was particularly impressed by the woman in the group, older than I and without a computer or Internet service, who presented so much information. Overall, I thought the evening had been a success, and I felt as if I had made a huge first step.

Fortified by that initial effort, I located a social group in my small town through Meetup and RSVP'd to a dinner and movie the following weekend. Ironically, Meetup had been at the top of my list of things to do when we had arrived in our new state. However, I had never had a need for connection at the time, because of the frequent activities in our neighborhood in which we participated. Again, all were friendly and welcoming. I suddenly had the prospect of a social life.

I returned to the book club the following month and learned it had a "think tank" that met once a month to discuss current events and controversial topics, ranging from political campaigning to the demise of the family, as well as the lack of equal opportunities for women in business and in the world at large. I attended that, too, and while some of the people were also in the book club, I saw new faces as well. This group had also been together some time, so it was easy for me to allow them to carry the conversation while I just sat and absorbed the experience. I had been praying for women friends, and it turned out they had always been there.

I felt like a prisoner stepping into the sunshine after a long confinement, and I wanted more. I made myself embrace the opportunity to discover friends, and I began to cautiously and judiciously share my story. I signed up for a square-dancing lesson, chocolate making, and a psychic reading. Many years before, my younger daughter and I had been curious and had scheduled a psychic reading. We had both been doubtful about the legitimacy or the outcome but had been equally impressed by the insights we'd received. Now seemed an appropriate time for another reading. I certainly had nothing to lose. I had no need for conversation with the psychic, as she uncannily laid my recent existence before me and outlined a future for me on her own. I was determined to provide no clues and, having a very limited amount of time, eager to discover what she might have to say.

When I was shown to her private room, she appeared quite fidgety and reminded me of a first-grader in desperate need of a bathroom. She quickly asked, "How do you want to begin?"

I suggested, "Perhaps you should begin, as you seem anxious to share."

She immediately blurted, "There is a serious male aura that surrounds you."

I explained, "My father has just died."

She suggested, "It's more than that."

I supplied, "I'm recently separated."

"That's it! You have no closure!" With no prompting, she went on. "Your life is unfolding, and I see you in a beautiful garden that you are not enjoying. You are unable to enjoy where you are because you feel as if perhaps you should be somewhere else. Your daughters will both be fine. Attend to the garden you have been provided here, and take note of the beauty that surrounds you."

The accuracy of her insights revealed how easily she had seen into the depths of my soul. Returning to the group, I mingled a bit before excusing myself to begin the drive home and to contemplate what I had just been told.

After that, I went to theater openings; participated in house, garden, and island tours; and tried cocktails and food at new restaurants all over town. I selected a variety of events that would provide new and unique experiences. Each, however, held a commonality: none of the selected venues would require intimate or extended conversation from me.

I was often nervous, and on occasion either left an event quite early or canceled altogether. In adopting Lucy, I realized with crystal clarity, I had gained more than just her companionship. As a puppy, she provided a repertoire of legitimate demands requiring attention. It was easy to excuse myself from an event and head home early. I could avoid extended time spent with others or the suggestion to follow up an activity with dinner or drinks. After all, I was now a pet owner and Lucy was at home, waiting to be fed or walked.

However, after each new attempt, my apprehension lessened, my geographic knowledge of the area in which I lived expanded, and my confidence began to grow. I even ventured back to neighborhood gatherings, although at a much slower pace. Again, this did not go flawlessly. My first effort found me at a costume party in the home of a friend. I was extremely apprehensive about attending this event, as it was my first outing where I would be single in a room filled with couples. I had declined the offers to attend several times, but my friend was supportive and persistent. "Come. You know everyone, and you're always a welcome guest." There was nothing I wanted to do less than attend a Halloween party. Even as a child, I had never enjoyed the holiday. As an adult, I always made plans to be away from the house, so as not to have to pass out candy, and I didn't dress in costume. However, her kind insistence that I attend wore me down and made me feel confident that I could accomplish this next step. I did, however, make a promise to myself and the hostess: "I will make only a brief appearance."

I was the first guest to arrive, and a glass of wine was poured and placed in my hand. Admiring their new kitchen renovation, I commented on what a difference the changed layout made in the space. I mentioned, "I ran three miles at the fitness center this morning."

Both offered, "Congratulations." I clutched my glass of wine, continued to exchange idle chitchat with her and her spouse, and believed that everything was going smoothly. I marveled at how well I was doing in the situation as more and more neighbors and friends arrived. I admired the creativity of their costumes and was particularly impressed with the husband who owned a nursery and appeared as a watering can, while his wife was dressed as a flowering plant. My confidence began to diminish, however, as we approached the moment to document the festivities with a picture. I was flooded with memories as each person scrambled to pair with their spouse. I stood there alone, recalling a time not so long ago, when my partner would search longingly for me and grasp my waist eagerly as we posed.

Suddenly, I experienced unexpected shortness of breath, dizziness, and weakness in my knees as I found myself surrounded by couples with whom we had shared so much. Mingling once again with people who knew me only as one half of a couple was too much for me to handle, and I went limp with despair. One of the women escorted me to my vehicle, questioning my ability to drive and probing for reasons why I had reacted in such a way. I settled myself behind the wheel without speaking. My heart was pounding, my skin clammy, but somehow I made my way safely around the corner. I pulled into the garage, sent Lucy out to the backyard to take care of her evening business, and crawled shakily into my bed, hoping for sleep.

∽

THE FOLLOWING DAY I discussed my dreadful experience with my therapist. She confirmed what I had expected. I had experienced my first—and, I hoped, my last—panic attack. I weighed each subsequent invitation carefully, and accepted them with preplanned escape routes and unconfined spaces in mind. I tried different experiences and explored different connections.

Outdoor gatherings and family parties where children were present were far less threatening. I attended small gatherings of women only. I moved carefully as I inched back into the pool of social interaction. Again, I relied on the strength and support of my friends Robbie and Mary-Ann to nudge me forward. I was in Charleston, Robbie in Atlanta, and Mary-Ann in Chicago, yet each provided support with daily phone calls and texts, making me feel as if they were just next door. They watched and encouraged me as I sent them pictures or videos of my selection of outfits for each event. Often, they talked to me on the phone as I drove toward my destination, after I had texted that I had no strength to step out of the house. They clearly understood I could no longer continue to live as I had been living. I had to move ahead. I had to expand my world. I had to rebuild my life.

As is often the case, adversity had provided opportunity. Loss had provided renewal. The experience with my neighbor forced me onward. Meeting new people helped reduce my anxiety and build my confidence. As I settled into a place where people were once again available, I realized I didn't need an endless array of individuals in my life. That was not my style. To me, friendship was a deep commitment, and it required a great deal of time and effort. I needed just a few good friends whom I could call upon in good times or in bad.

The time I spent with Audrey and her children afforded

me the support and love of a wider family circle. My connection to and love for her deepened as our relationship expanded. She and I developed a routine of having long weekly telephone conversations, during which we reminded each other that we both had to eat. We reminisced about the man we both loved dearly, who had left such emptiness behind. We shared stories of our memories of that man, and we clung to the connection that we enjoyed because he had been in our lives. I grew to rely on her insights and seek her guidance. I flew to visit her again in Indiana, and she excitedly made plans to fly to visit me as soon as she was able.

Time with dear friends and my own relatives, many of whom I hadn't seen in years, reminded me of the strength of the bonds I shared with others. I learned of family stories I had never heard and listened to people I had never met speak of undying respect and lasting love for the father I had lost. I cherished every story, every anecdote, and every opportunity to learn more about him and to embrace all that I had gained from having him in my life. Even in mourning, I was feeling his strength. Feeling that, perhaps, I would not always be punched back down. Feeling that, indeed, I could go on.

CHAPTER EIGHT

⟨⟩

What Made You Think This Would End Any Other Way?

"We define ourselves not through what we reveal, but what we hide."
—AZAR NAFISI, *THINGS I'VE BEEN SILENT ABOUT*

I WAS SHOCKED AND HURT THE FIRST TIME I HEARD it, but perhaps my therapist was correct. Looking back, I should perhaps have seen it coming. Surely there were signs. I had always placed him on a pedestal, assured him he was one in a million, the one every woman would pick from a room filled with men. I had thought myself fortunate for his kindness and calm, and for the selflessness I thought he had provided to his first wife and to our relationship. I had believed all his words, had taken everything at face value, and was caught completely off guard. A friend told me, "People don't change. Some are just better at hiding their real identity."

Four years later, over a glass of wine and quiet reflection on my long and difficult journey, the same friend expounded, "I never got a warm feeling from him." I had certainly heard that comment before. She went on to explain that her husband, upon meeting mine for the first time, later commented that he was a "snake in the grass." How had I been so blind? The truth was, I never saw it coming. I was the last one to see the relationship unfolding, and I was the last to know that it was collapsing.

We were different people with different needs and fears. He needed constant nurturing and feared abandonment. I needed independence and space and feared suffocation. He was absent-minded and always taking shortcuts. I was thorough, organized, and efficient. Were we incapable of meshing? I had insisted he take time to find himself after his divorce, and perhaps that time of separation was what had caused a breach. He had been angry but had assured me that his soul searching had been a success and presented as a healthier and happier version of himself. Had he held a hidden grudge? His children had never fully accepted our relationship. They had never known their parents had problems. Consequently, I had appeared to be the cause of the breakup of their marriage. Were their fears an issue?

While I had resisted involvement with him at the beginning, I had embraced the idea of second chances, and when I committed, I committed fully. Perhaps my initial reluctance was an unconscious warning. I blended him into my life and my household, even though he contributed very little and gave most of his belongings to his daughter. I worked hard to assimilate his adult children into our lives. I became attuned to their personal tastes in foods, household temperature, and individual quirks. I stood with the family when his son enlisted in the Marines and completed basic training. I was there to say goodbye when he was deployed to Iraq as he gave me a huge hug and whispered to me, "Please take care of Dad." I sent letters to him on whimsical paper each day he was away. I welcomed him home, honoring his accomplishments and service.

I embraced their friends and love interests, attended their graduations and weddings, and prepared for and hosted all holidays. It was I who suggested gift ideas, purchased those items, and typically even did the wrapping. I spent weeks meticulously laboring over personalized cross-stitched baby samplers for newborns, and I had been diligently working on the third such gift for the infant due shortly after he left. I prepared and froze favorite foods at the births of those children and left those items in their freezers when we departed, after supporting the new parents in their transition when the babies came home. I established the tradition of juvenile-size wooden rocking chairs made by a local artisan for first birthdays, hoping they would later become family heirlooms. I even provided airfare for a surprise visit from his daughter and grandson when it was otherwise impossible to get away to see them.

Time lessened lingering concerns regarding the feeling that the other shoe would drop. I became convinced that he was indeed "in it for life," as he insisted. I was certain that this love, this marriage, this relationship would end only with death.

Neither he nor I was perfect. However, our relationship was very close and grew increasingly secure with each passing day. Our conversations centered on a growing love and commitment, and those conversations far outnumbered any that mentioned concerns. Outsiders, as well as close friends and family, saw a couple that worked. We were comfortable and carefree with each other, an easy fit. His departure shocked all but the most perceptive and raised doubts and confusion in others when they learned he had walked away. Therapists, my attorney, and one friend unsurprisingly and objectively assessed the circumstances. Most, and mostly I myself, were horrified and felt betrayed by the collapse of a marriage as seemingly strong as ours.

Reflecting on the life we had shared, I realized that we had not shared a life at all. He had absorbed my life into his. He had eagerly incorporated my traditions and celebrations. He had greedily stepped into the world I had created—including my daughters and my friends—until he was ready to move on. Had we only been playing at a relationship? Were the vacations, weekends, dates, conversations, and fun only an illusion? We had done so much and had such a variety of experiences. We had shared family gatherings, concerts, plays, travel, movies, weddings, and births. We had hosted dinner parties and barbecues. We had taken cooking lessons. Yet, outside the bedroom, I saw his smile only at the birth of his two grandsons and on other rare, isolated occasions. He would never applaud at entertainment venues, never stand for an ovation. Were those red flags? Perhaps the communication on which we prided ourselves had never really been honest. Perhaps he just couldn't be happy.

Perhaps he had taken all that he needed. I was reminded of a time in my childhood when I had been playing at a nearby creek with my neighborhood friends. A leech had attached itself to my thigh and refused to release me from its grasp. I watched as it increased in size and strength, sucking the blood from my limb, until it was successfully removed and I was free. Like the leech, my husband had attached himself to me and determinedly succeeded in sucking the life from me.

I had been certain he had discovered in me a new wife, one whom he found a little smarter, a little prettier, a little more adventurous—both in and out of the bedroom—and with a little more drive and backbone than the first. Perhaps he had been relying on my strength to maintain his personal and professional growth and was worn down over time as he realized he had none of his own. Perhaps I had come to enjoy being needed, when what I really needed was to be me. Perhaps I didn't realize I had been losing myself until I began to once again explore social opportunities and to discover how lost I had become. Perhaps it is human nature that even when there are concerns, we see what we want to see and close our eyes to the rest.

I realized, with a new emotional strength and increased perspective, I may have missed some obvious indicators of the disaster and pain. One was likely during the ride to the hotel with my girls on the day of our wedding. It had been difficult to drive, as I had struggled to avoid hyperventilation. Suddenly questioning the sanity of the situation, I had been filled with only trepidation, which, at the time, I had overlooked. Perhaps the fact that when we entered the room for the ceremony, where he and his children were already gathered, Jim had a glass of wine in his hand and had already begun drinking. Was that a sign? At the time, I thought it only nerves. Had it been something else? Had he been having second thoughts? Had he been fearful of giving marriage another chance? Was he already questioning his decision to pursue and conquer me?

I have learned to recognize that his behavior was inconsistent with his feelings and I was merely a part of his plan. I was one of many. I have come to believe I was merely a stepping-stone along his path of taking what he needed from a relationship and then moving on. Yet, at the time, I never saw it coming. I never had a clue it would end the way it did. I had heard for years his repeated refrains of undying love. He assured me each day of his passion for and commitment to our marriage. He expressed wishes that I might understand and experience, if only briefly, the depth of what he felt for me. He reminded me frequently that, despite the passage of so many years, I continued to take his breath away. I often wondered if this was all exaggeration, but I never questioned the underlying truth of his words. After all, I still believed that I was a better person because he was in my life.

I still felt blindsided and confused about how the man I thought I knew so well could have betrayed me. If he had deemed his first wife stupid and described me as mean, what would be his criticism of the next? I was certain of only two things: he would take no responsibility for the termination of our marriage, and what I had thought we had was not love. He knew I had difficulty detecting manipulation, as it was not a tactic I used in my relationships. He played on my emotional vulnerability about marriage and offered all the right words. He knew full well that I would internalize responsibility for the collapse of our union and accept the shame and the guilt he would heap upon me when he was ready to leave.

He introduced a new phrase as he walked out the door: "It is what it is." While I remained uncertain about its actual meaning, it came to clearly identify my new life. Reflections on the time, the circumstances, the miscues, the responsibility, and the fault provided no understanding. "It is what it is." There was no going back. If granted a do-over, would I take it? I would not. After four long years with absolutely no communication, I had finally come to realize he undoubtedly had never been committed to our relationship. I was better off alone. If he had truly been unhappy and had clearly stated his issues, I would, of course, have worked toward a stronger and improved marriage and the resolution of his concerns. But even if he had voiced legitimate worries and responsibly worked toward resolution within the marriage, could I have been any better off than I am at this moment?

When one has lost everything, everything must be re-evaluated. It is said that hindsight is twenty-twenty. Would I have made different choices? If we had never moved and stayed where we were, I would have remained secure in my job, my home, and my friends. My daughters would have been nearby. He would still have left, but in that scenario, with a safety net in place, would my pain have been as deep? Would my experiences have been as sharp? Would my gain have been so monumental? Would I even have had the time to experience and process the loss I was experiencing and what was happening in my life? Would I have had the opportunity to learn as much, grow as much, and develop as completely as I have? I have become confident in my surroundings. I have stepped out of my comfort zone. I have experienced no more anxiety attacks. My path remains somewhat unclear, but of one thing I remain certain: I will continue to move ahead. I had been content without a shared life before he proclaimed his "infinite patience" and "lifelong love" for me. I would be content on my own once again. I would find my way, and I, like my tulips, would continue to grow and thrive.

CHAPTER NINE

❦

Who Are You, and What Are You Thinking?

"Never give up, for that is just the place and time the tide will turn."
—HARRIET BEECHER STOWE

*A*BOUT THE TIME HE LEFT, I HAD A NEIGHBOR who posted something on Facebook to this effect: "When a door closes, stop trying to beat it down and accept that you are not meant to have what is behind it."

I had certainly been pounding on that door. I wanted what had been taken returned to me. I had internalized responsibility for every bit of the guilt and blame he piled upon me. I used any lucid moments I experienced to try to reach out, to make sense, to formulate plans, and to compile options. My efforts to communicate went mostly unheeded. Calls made to his office went directly to his secretary. When he did answer, I suggested, "Let's find a time when we can talk and clear this up. Avoiding each other just allows us to stew in our own juices. We can figure this out."

He responded, "I'm happy stewing in my juices. I've found a therapist, and she told me people like you are unable to love."

That seemed like an unusual and unwarranted statement.

My therapist had never conveyed hostility toward or generalizations about him. Her only goal was to assist me in working through my grief. A friend who had closely observed my journey through my first divorce had asked me, "Why aren't you angry?"

I explained, "Anger only hurts me. He doesn't care if I'm angry, and I gain nothing from allowing it into my life."

She suggested, "If you won't be angry, then you must determine what it is you are to learn from this."

I was trying to do just that. I filled every waking moment with the sound bite of the words he had said—the accusations of cruelty, and his insistence that he had told me repeatedly about how he had felt. How had I never heard any of these dialogues he insisted took place? I could clearly recall the persistent, hissing voice that told me I was vile and undeserving of conversation, and that our marriage was over, and it left me completely distraught. When I wasn't replaying his voice and his words in my head, I was still attempting to call, to beg, to apologize, to explain. Often, I was writing, but always I was absorbing blame, always hoping that the life we had shared could be salvaged.

I knew that marriages crumble and that love ends, but not in a weekend. I understood that there were endless scenarios involving the loss of a loved one: random accidents, lingering illness, suicide, a heart attack. I felt certain the most painful was the unexpected, especially the abandonment. He told me that I was mean and filed court papers saying that and more. He stopped just short of using vulgar language to describe my evil behavior and my full responsibility in causing the end of our marriage. The document was so scathing and unexpected that my attorney contacted me immediately before forwarding the document on to me. In an effort to deflect the impact and to soften the blow, she reminded me, "Keep in mind who sent it." She needn't have worried. The file was so ridiculous in its presentation and tone, even I could not take it seriously. Still, she then contacted his attorney and told him, "Under no circumstances will my client meet face-to-face with your client." Continuing on, she reprimanded him: "Shame on you! That was unfounded, unnecessary, and unprofessional."

The response was quick: "We do not have anything else. We have no grounds for this divorce, no motives on which to file." His reasons did not matter. Our marriage was over, the betrayal unexpected, the wound deep. The handling was needlessly hurtful and left a permanent scar. I often wondered just what he said to people. How did he face himself in the mirror each morning? What was his justification?

"Mean"? What a childish and intangible word. I had heard more expressive accusations from the first-graders I had taught. Even if it had been true, which I knew with certainty it was not, did I deserve to be treated so despicably? I had worked hard to blend our families, to provide a welcoming home for all. I had been selfless in my love. I had retired and relocated. I had sold my home only months before. Did I—did anyone—deserve such disrespect and unconcealed loathing and animosity? Did I deserve to be left to clean up the detritus of the life he had left behind? Surely, a woman who was mean would have simply trashed his belongings, rather than storing them until it was convenient for him to pick them up.

After he left, I had ordered and read Gary Chapman's book *The Five Love Languages*. It has been studied and documented that men will not leave a relationship without having established a new one into which to move. Even a cursory Google search indicates that men have a backup plan in place before moving on. As I look back, I realize that is just what he did with me when he was leaving his first wife, although I never felt that way at the time. I was certain it was our proximity, a shared commonality with our children, and the unraveling of his marriage that brought us together, but perhaps I was just a safe and convenient place to land. My attorney had encouraged the hiring of a private investigator, but I had declined. What good could come of it? A quicker divorce? What change could it make? He would never have forgiven such an act, and at the time I received the suggestion, I held out hope for a reconciliation. As my daughter told me early on, "If he has opted out, there is nothing you can do to opt him back in." Divorce is difficult. Loss is painful and lonely. I knew this from the first time I divorced. I knew what to expect, and I knew it wouldn't be easy. It turned out I knew nothing at all.

Weeks turned into months without contact or communication. He continued to pay bills electronically, and I continued to use our debit card to provide for myself. His mail continued to arrive at our shared address, until I suggested, via email, our only communication, that he change his mailing address. Also via email, an offer from him arrived after the receipt of disclosure documents from our attorneys. While sitting at a favorite local eatery with a friend one day, I received word that he suddenly wanted to talk. He insisted that we could work through a settlement without the aid of lawyers and assured me that he had a plan in place. He offered to meet and buy my lunch. I reminded him that we had not communicated in months and that attorneys were already in place, and I declined. He shared his plan with me nevertheless.

He assured me that his pension plan had nothing available and that his 401(k) portfolio was nominal at best after the 2008 recession. He offered to provide me with $600 per month spousal support until I was sixty-two (fourteen months away).

He suggested I could then collect my Social Security benefit. He assigned a generous $8,400 value to my contributions to our marriage and his success. Six hundred dollars per month, or even the $840 per month reduced Social Security benefit, would not cover food and utilities, not to mention mortgage or rental payments. I had no job and no income to supplement such an outlandish and demeaning offer, even if I had been foolish enough to give it consideration. I had retired to relocate and to support him. While he may have been planning this break for some time, the situation was new to me. I needed time. Unbeknownst to him, I knew the exact balance of his 401(k) portfolio, and it was far beyond nominal. Indeed, I had made copies. I had also copied and supplied to my attorney tax returns and pension fund statements. There was no hiding the fact that we had significant assets that would need to be divided equitably.

So, time dragged on: attorneys were hired, documents filed, delays, delays, delays. He fired his first lawyer. Although we never discussed the rationale for his decision, his second choice was a respected and recognized name in the field of family law. He was a more formidable contender, and it likely pained him to pay for the expertise he brought to the table when the two representatives faced off. Deaths, illness, and injuries occurred, causing more postponements. He remained adamant that his offer was fair and justified, and was unwilling to negotiate.

Attorneys for both sides continued to argue about an adjusted offer. Frustrations mounted as time continued to pass and fees continued to accumulate for each of us. Hostilities increased as each side held the other responsible for the continued deadlock and delay. Telephone and face-to-face planning and reporting meetings occurred between the lawyers. Two years dragged by before the mandatory mediation even grew near, and neither side was hopeful that the process would succeed. I had to miss Christmas with my daughters because of mediation scheduling. I signed up for holiday cooking and painting classes to fill the void left by the absence of time spent with them.

I sent Lucy to puppy day care on the appointed day, with emergency stipulations for overnight boarding if mediation continued beyond closing. Her crate, typically a fixture in the cargo area of my vehicle, was removed. I wanted him to have no knowledge of anything that was currently happening in my life. Traffic across the Charleston bridges that I would need to traverse in order to arrive punctually at mediation was unpredictable even in good weather. Therefore, I allowed plenty of time for my journey.

I was the first to arrive at the mediation office, where I began to unpack and settle in. I had known the room would be cold, and I had dressed in leggings and knee-high rain boots. I had also donned a camisole, tunic, additional sweater wrap, neck scarf, and full-length, lined raincoat. I began to make our space as cozy as possible for all. It would be a long day, and I wanted my team to be comfortable. I placed Christmas-red tulips in a vase, lit a scented holiday votive, and spread cocktail napkins about. I had baked cookies, cinnamon rolls, and fudge for all to share. Of course I had also brought my recently acquired tablet, which would later be put to good use as negotiations dragged on.

He and his attorney arrived quite late, not only delaying proceedings but also casting additional doubt on the possibility of our attaining a resolution. As we awaited their arrival, the mediator introduced himself and looked at me, saying, "Tell me two things about your spouse that I don't know from these documents."

That was easy, and my response was quick. "He thinks that attorneys are bottom-feeders." Then I added, "He was also born with a slight disability. His right arm is a bit too short, and he is unable to reach into his back pocket for his wallet." Asking for permission to add a third bit of insight, I received it immediately. "He does not go by the name on those documents. Although Jimmy is indeed his given name, it is used only by family members—that is, except for his sister. She calls him Snook."

An immediate and mischievous grin spread across the mediator's face. Looking directly at me, he responded, "I shall think of him only as Snook throughout this mediation process."

Although I knew he would be asking the same question as he entered the room to meet my husband and his attorney, I relaxed momentarily. I felt confident that a meaningful alliance had been formed, one that might help ease the frustration of the long day that lay ahead.

Mediation in South Carolina is not what we see on TV. There are no brightly lit rooms with cozy chairs in which all involved sit around a gleaming table to air their concerns and work through their issues. Compromise and consensus are not reached quickly. Opposing sides are kept apart. As we settled into separate rooms with our respective teams, the skies opened early and thunderstorms hit hard. I had instructed my attorney that I wanted to terminate mediation if we reached a standstill, and by late morning I held out little hope. When we ordered lunch, the soup and pasta I had forced down caused immediate rumblings. I asked my team and the mediator, "Have any clients ever had to vomit during this process?" They assured me that it happened all the time and brought to my attention a conveniently placed wastebasket in the corner. I was not one to humiliate myself by publicly throwing up and was immediately escorted to a private restroom. The mediator returned to where my husband sat with his attorney, and the other team was kept locked down in their respective room until I could compose myself.

As day turned into evening, fatigue settled in. He began to budge on support but was insistent that I owed him for monies spent during our marriage. Hours continued to pass as the mediator moved between the rooms. I was fighting back tears and working through budget scenarios on my tablet with my CPA. It seemed to me that whatever numbers we keyed into the budget, the life I had known was about to change dramatically. I was worried that this onslaught would never end.

Suddenly, a modern-day miracle again occurred in my life. As the mediator reentered our room, he sat down across the table from me, brought his chair in close, and looked me directly in the eye. "I think we may have a deal. He has relinquished the battle for repayment of expenses incurred during the marriage. He will meet our number on monthly support. He will continue to pay all of your household expenses through May. And, if you are willing, the house will be completely yours."

I couldn't believe what I was hearing. Just moments earlier, I had been wondering where and how I would live. Unexpectedly, money issues were now seemingly resolved, and the home would be mine. There would be no requirement to list or sell it. I would not be expected to move. I would not have to split the equity. It was all mine, with only the stipulation that I have it refinanced in just my own name by the following May. Gazing around the table at my team, I saw that we all shared the same perplexed but relieved looks.

Yet his turning over the house made perfect sense from my perspective. He had never been involved in anything to do with our home, aside from paying the mortgage and mowing the lawn. He had shown little interest in its purchase or enthusiasm for its decor. He would certainly not want to take any responsibility for the sale. Details were finalized and documents collected, and he and his lawyer were shown out. When the parking lot was empty and I could be escorted to my vehicle without fear of confrontation, we exchanged hugs around my table, enthusiastic holiday greetings, and recipes for the treats I had shared. The day's final advice from my attorney was, "Go and get Lucy. Get home safely, open a bottle of wine in front of the fire, and relax. It's over."

I climbed into my car and rechecked the seat and the mirror adjustments as bad weather confronted me once again. As I drove home in a deluge, I found myself focusing once more on my personal safety. I gripped the wheel and concentrated on my destination. Good fortune allowed me to pick up Lucy, and, with dog in tow, I headed home. When I arrived, I put her outside and exchanged my wet clothes for warm and comfortable pajamas. I dried Lucy and brought her back inside, where a cozy fire, a lighted Christmas tree, and scented candles awaited. I opened a bottle of wine and made my promised call to Robbie to tell her that it was over. I was unable to offer much information. I needed time to sort through all the documents, as well as my own emotions, before I could fully understand them and explain what had occurred and how it had happened. But for now, I could relax.

As I hung up the phone and sipped my only glass of wine, exhaustion overcame me. Final papers would be prepared and signed in court the first week of June. The delay was deliberate, as that date marked a long-term marriage that had lasted ten years. It would assure me of my share of his Social Security benefits. When that day arrived, neither he nor his attorney would be in court. An associate from the law firm would handle the final phase, and the judge would wonder why that was so. My attorney and I were not surprised. He and his attorney would have had to appear like naughty puppies with their tails between their legs for all of the hostility and inhumanity they had displayed over the two years it had taken to come that far.

Still, for the time being, it was behind me. I could focus my energies on rebuilding my independent and unchartered life. I had experienced pain and loss that had been both unexpected and unimaginable. The road I had traveled had appeared un-navigable, but, with support, I had reached the end. I was unsure of what lay ahead or the path I would take, but of one thing I was certain: I had survived. Now that both shoes had dropped, I could confidently choose a new pair and fashion a new path, one step at a time. Perhaps I would select dancing shoes—perhaps ruby slippers, like Dorothy wore. I would click my heels three times and be transported to the place of which I had been dreaming—the place that I would know was home. Whatever the shoes, I would blaze my own trail, rather than following the one laid out precariously by someone else. I would choreograph a new life and realize new dreams. I would never be the same, but I was determined to be even better than I had been before. But for now, it was time to put this day behind me and head to bed for some much-needed sleep.

CHAPTER TEN

Moving On

"[But] it's no use going back to yesterday,
for I was a different person then."

—LEWIS CARROLL, *ALICE'S ADVENTURE IN WONDERLAND*

*I*T IS EARLY SATURDAY MORNING ON ANOTHER spring weekend in April, but four years have passed. Lucy has been let out, has finished her breakfast, and lies, lazy and contented, on her bed in front of the fire. Nearly two years have gone by since I was sent home from mediation and assured, "It's over." I have worked diligently at rebuilding my life. My sparkle has returned, and it is contingent only upon me. There is an effortless cadence and new serenity to each day since the reality of my healing made me whole once again. Each day, and every choice I make regarding how to fill it, belongs only to me. I long ago stopped wishing for the phone to ring or for the voice mail light to blink, indicating a message from him. I have grown accustomed to questioning looks from casual acquaintances wondering why I am still here. Because I no longer need to spend every ounce of my energy focused on healing, divorce, and survival, I can quickly address the routine challenges of daily life. They no longer seem like insurmountable obstacles.

My refrigerator remains essentially empty. Having never prioritized food, I still eat little, but what I eat stays down. Meal preparation is sporadic, and cooking for one remains a challenge. Occasionally, I invite friends over for dinner or a luncheon because I do enjoy the experience of cooking. Surprisingly, I have found myself trying to take an interest in looking at new recipes, and, while I rarely follow through, at times I even prepare a meal. I stopped using the dishwasher long ago. It took so long to fill, the items I placed inside it began to smell and it was much more efficient and pleasurable just to hand-wash any dishes I had used.

I have also changed my name, reverting to the English translation of the Polish name I was given at birth. I shared my plan with my family early on in this journey, and my father and my daughters were in full support. My new name is on all of my documents, accounts, and Social Security profile. I have finalized my will and established trusts for myself and my daughters. Whatever I have has been protected and will go directly and exclusively to them. I have secured the details of my life and death. My daughters have brought me nothing but joy, and I hope never to burden them. I have made every effort to leave nothing to chance.

Grief was my prison, loss my captor. They were both difficult to escape and required all my strength, as well as the aid of my family and friends to move beyond the walls of confinement. Still, I often stumbled and fell back. I had days when I felt driven and compelled to move forward, only to then experience isolation, loneliness, and a sense of being trapped. New friendships and connections were slow to develop and required time to grow.

I found that unexpectedly starting over, alone, at sixty, and trying to create and build a new life was far more difficult than it had been at forty, when I had children on whom to rely for motivation and purpose. But, at last, I have patiently established a genuine sense of community. I have made new friends and connections, and I eagerly anticipate my daily interactions with the people whom I have come to know and value. When they are aware of my absence, they follow up with questions and concerns regarding my safety and well-being as I do for them.

My days are full and contain much meaning. I continue to watch my daughters, now in their thirties, grow into their own and overcome their own obstacles. I bask in the shared moments and experiences I have with them. I delight in the pleasure it brings to my heart to know that they want me in their lives. I look forward to the concerts, holidays, vacations, and special visits we share. I have a life filled with peace and joy—the joy a dear friend consistently prayed would find me. Aside from my career, from which I retired to relocate, my grandchildren, whom I selflessly relinquished, even though I cherished them more than words can express, and my geographic proximity to my daughters, I have regained all that I sacrificed in the name of love and commitment. I would like nothing more than to have my daughters close by. I miss having them drop in on their way home from work, or calling to arrange time for shopping and lunch. I miss our routine and our history of shared holidays and daily interactions, and I often consider the possibility of returning to be near them. When I think of them, I experience a sense of total confusion regarding just where I ought to live. It is unclear whether I will ultimately be able to stay or go. However, it is too soon right now to make that decision. I am newly healed, and I am experiencing something completely foreign to me. For the first time in my life, I have only to think of myself and what I want from life.

I am still uncertain about how my future will unfold, but for now I will remain where I am and continue to reside at my current location. I am comfortable in the world I have created and even enjoy sleeping alone and undisturbed each night. I have rediscovered a balance in my life and focus on living day by day—although I sometimes still rely on cues in my journal or my daily calendar to remind me to focus on those important concepts.

I had always been one who celebrated life—the clinking of glasses, bubbles in the tub, birds at a feeder. Although he did not understand the value of these little pleasures, I have continued to enjoy them. Each provides a sense of peace, joy, and appreciation of the world, which I want always to acknowledge. As I made each small gain in my journey, I had a tiny celebration. I purchased two new wineglasses when my divorce was final, two new coffee mugs when I refinanced my home and the house was legally mine. I shredded my journals. I pampered myself in meaningful, not extravagant, ways. Some found my behavior pretentious. Some found it unnecessary. Trite or trivial, pretentious or not, that is who I am and who I will remain.

I am determined to waste not one more moment of this precious life I have been given. I am grateful that he chose to leave and, in so doing, opened so many doors. Because he did, I have become fearless and eager to move on. I have realized through writing what a difficult and isolated road I traveled. Four years is too much time to have spent in the search for understanding, and I am more than ready to put that experience behind me. I have, at last, left my pain behind. I have accomplished my goal, with no residual emotion, regret, nostalgia, or concern over the why, what, when, or how of my former relationship.

I never anticipated, imagined, or could have foreseen that by giving up myself, I would in fact discover exactly who I am. I am finding my stride and enjoying my newfound freedom and the new friends, new opportunities, new independence, and new life it has provided. I am no longer lost; I have found myself once again. And I have discovered that much of what once seemed so important holds little value. I am pleasantly content and at peace in my new life, in my home with my pup, my tulips, and my wine, which I now enjoy in celebration, not self-medicated escape.

I recently completed my final purging process and treated myself, yet again, to small indulgences. I have purchased a new headboard, updated my bedding, and installed new light fixtures, which my husband would not have supported. I have swapped rugs and picture frames from room to room, and each little change has had a huge impact on the growing feeling that I am truly living my life the way I want to live it. I understand beyond a doubt that my home is an integral part of my health and well-being. Its size, location, or appointments are not what matter; it is the love, family, and serenity that reside there. I need a place that is a haven for me, a place where I can be me and where I can embrace those who matter—and will grow to matter—in my life.

I have returned to beginning and ending my day with music and the inspiration that it provides. As I recently strolled along my favorite beach on an unseasonably warm and pleasant day, I clearly realized that life is not about endings, but about beginnings. I know that for each chapter that closes, another chapter awaits. I know I will return to this beach and discover new treasures there. I understand that with luck, strength, support, and time, the more we lose, the more fearless we become. That life really is good.

I have stretched beyond any limits or boundaries I ever anticipated. I know that each person I may encounter on any day is at a very different place than I. I realize that to expect anyone to meet or understand my needs when they are in a different place sets me up for misunderstanding, bitterness, resentment, and disappointment.

I have challenged myself with new social situations and pushed myself out of the unstructured leisure of retirement to discover a new opportunity, and the realization of a lifelong dream, in writing. Amazingly, I have relied only on myself for the first time ever. I have embraced life and everything it has and will continue to offer. I have accomplished more than I ever imagined I could on my own. I have risen above unimaginable obstacles.

This book began as an immediate and instantaneous response to the most painfully unexpected experience of my life. Having regularly found answers in books, I hoped that this time, writing one of my own would help me discover answers to the hardest questions I had ever faced—those I didn't even know I needed to ask. Sitting on the beach, I began scribbling ideas, thoughts, and chapter titles. Notes were added and collected over more than four years of writing during sleepless nights and rare lucid moments. Fingers and bedsheets became covered in ink dots as I repeatedly opened and closed the pen that remained close by to scribble thoughts onto paper as words floated through my head in the dark of night.

I sit, pen in hand, with a steaming mug of coffee and the sun about to rise. There is the promise of another glorious day, and I am awash with emotion. I have accomplished my goals.

The story has been submitted and accepted for publication. In less than a month, I will visit with both of my daughters and have time with my best friend as we celebrate birthdays and the coming of spring. He may have been finished, but I was only beginning.

And as time has passed, I have gained a new perspective. I am able to step back and see, with an altered view, that even the most irregular pieces of this most complicated puzzle have finally fallen into place.

He had been involved with someone else and had been looking for a way to escape our marriage. The man who was "instantly intrigued" and "had to know" me became intrigued by someone else and had to know her. He had married yet again, to the woman he had sworn was not in his life. The young man who came to assist him in loading his belongings was indeed her son. Learning of his new situation through a random post on social media, I was overcome by unexpected emotion, but not by the emotion that one might expect. I felt a liberating sense of relief. The discovery of this information provided the confirmation of what I had always known. He had been involved with someone else and had been looking for a way to escape our marriage.

The signs I had missed along the way became readily apparent. The spin I had assigned to his actions and words took on different meaning. I felt embarrassed by my foolishness. I had been completely gullible. When we moved to South Carolina, he insisted I not sell my home. Yet he spinelessly allowed me to sell that house—and planned to invest the funds from the sale in a backyard pool in the place where we had decided to settle permanently—only months before he knew he would walk away. He knew from the time of our relocation the way our story would end. He never had my back. He knew all the motions and the right things to say to manipulate me. He was calculating and deliberate in his meek and mild demeanor and used my insecurities to his benefit. He had a grand plan to which I was not privy.

So it is now time to amend the story of us. "Once upon a time, a beautiful woman fell under the spell of a charming and handsome man. He whispered the most enchanting words and provided the most magical experiences—until one day, he told the woman that he was done and disappeared without a word. That woman was transformed by his leaving. That woman was me."

Epilogue

"Life must be lived forward but understood backward."
—KIERKEGAARD

*D*ivorce is devastating—especially to women. For those of us who are older, the resulting changes in financial security often force us to rely on investments or Social Security before we can obtain the full benefit of either. But I had angels watching over me, showing me the way, providing miracles in even my darkest times. I was one of the fortunate ones. I had a strong network of personal and professional support and remained financially secure. My therapist assured me that my network and my writing saved me. She told me that few people had the support I had. I had always thought friendships like mine were typical. I believed that what we put out came back to us, and that everyone had a network like mine in place. When I learned that was not the case, I was more grateful than ever before for what I had.

I was unsure of how or when it happened, but small, imperceptible changes began gradually taking place in my life and in my outlook. I noticed I was taking far more steps forward and far fewer steps backward. I realized the wrenching sadness and overwhelming loneliness of daily living and the emptiness of holidays alone—when I felt as if everyone else was happily involved with their spouses and their families—no longer surfaced. I was filled with genuine gratitude for my life, my daughters, my friends, and my health. Heartache gave way to hope, until one day I realized I felt an ongoing and consistent calm and a spreading and lasting joy. I had found peace and contentment in the life I had made. I had learned that it matters not *where* I am, but *who* I am.

I had discovered that beyond the healing, the greatest gift was the self-awareness I had gained through this process. I now clearly understand that real peace lies within and comes from remaining true to oneself. I know beyond a doubt that life can change in a moment and unexpected loss can occur at any time. I realize that after the passing of each day, fewer lie ahead, and I want to make the most of each one. The book has been completed, the story told. Throughout the experience, I struggled with the reasons and the lessons I was meant to learn. Even without gaining real understanding or closure regarding the end of my marriage, I realized I had gained so much.

I had learned that I had Herculean strength that I had never imagined. I often wanted to scream the words "I can't!" Instead, my mantra became "I *must*! There is no other choice!" I had been amazed by my resilience and capabilities, as well as by my strength in stretching my limits and exploring new options. I had discovered that all individuals can become superhuman by opening our minds and our hearts. I had learned the true depth of the human spirit. I had come to like and trust myself again and had realized that I was always a likable person. I learned to accept myself for who I am at this moment—not who I hope to be—and now make every effort to do the same for others who cross my path.

I have come full circle as I continue to rebuild my life. My journey has transported me to another place and time. I am filled with gratitude that I have come out of the darkness of doubt and know that life is a gift that should not be taken for granted—the most important lesson I have learned—and that I have healed. I clearly understand the meaning of resiliency and the compelling condition of the human spirit to overcome and move beyond even the most excruciating pain. I know first-hand that the experience of loss and the process of grief are unpredictable and as different as the individual struggling through them. I know that outsiders rarely understand that struggle and are usually capable of support for far too little time.

The writing process itself was like ocean waves that break upon the shore and carry away stale debris as they leave behind new treasures. I wanted my story told, but I wanted a story of hope, resiliency, optimism, strength, and new opportunities. Telling the story the way I wanted to has helped me, and it is my hope that it will help others experiencing similar situations.

I understand that the everyday challenges that try us are trivial and can be ignored. The big challenges are what require our strength and incite our growth, and seeking help is a strength, not a weakness. In fact, I believe it is imperative to secure professional help through individual counseling or a support group. My friends and family told me the same things that I heard from my therapist, and I appreciated and even re-quired their support and words for my very survival. Still, my innermost feeling was that they were encouraging me in such a way only because they loved me and cared about me on a very personal level. When I heard the same advice and statements repeated by a professional with no vested interest in me—aside from the income my visits provided—I could objectively accept what was being said and act upon the words, allowing myself to heal and grow. Divorce Care (www.divorcecare.org) offers support and caring across the world through email and per-sonal connections to people grieving the loss of a spouse.

I had read Elizabeth Gilbert's *Eat, Pray, Love* when it was first published, but at that time the pain of loss was an abstract fact for me. It is a wonderful chronicle of a woman searching to rebuild her life after the end of a relationship. I had clung to the insights of Jennifer Gilbert's journey through grief in *I Never Promised You a Goodie Bag*. While her loss was physically inflicted, her recovery, healing, and insights on grieving in American culture stayed with me and provided companionship on my long and lonely journey. Her quote opens my story, and I knew I wanted to be a better person after my experience than I had been before. I refused to allow bitterness or self-pity to have a place in my life. That was not the woman I would choose to be.

I was familiar with the five stages of grief and often repeated the Serenity Prayer to myself, knowing that there was much I could not change. I had friends, I had a therapist, but I still felt isolated, alone, and convinced that what I was experiencing was unique to my independent situation. I often found it difficult to discuss, as the shame that he had heaped upon me routinely resurfaced and overwhelmed me with guilt.

I had stumbled onto an excerpt of Sheryl Sandberg's recently published *Option B: Facing Adversity, Building Resilience, and Finding Joy* and had suggested it to a friend who had lost her son. In reading it myself, I discovered that there were specific names for what I was experiencing and strategies for coping with the loss and moving ahead. The ideas were enlightening and empowering. They would have been extremely beneficial if I had had them throughout my experience. In preparing my book for publication, I read the book *He's History, You're Not: Surviving Divorce After 40*, by Erica Manfred, which provides an excellent resource specifically targeting women in their forties, fifties, and sixties who are dealing with divorce. I highly recommend it.

The most personally compelling to me was the discovery of two books by Vikki Stark, which actually described and named the exact experience I was going through. They made me feel vindicated when I realized I was not alone and I was not at fault. *Runaway Husbands: The Abandoned Wife's Guide to Recovery and Renewal* and *Planet Heartbreak: Abandoned Wives Tell Their Stories* are a must-read for any woman who discovers herself in the pages of my story.

I felt abandoned and alone when he first announced that he was "fucking damn done," and I suspect that if you are reading this book, whatever your specific circumstances, you are experiencing similar feelings and emotions. While it is not within the scope of this book to outline, or even suggest, a sequence of healing for anyone aside from me, I can promise you that one thing is certain: regardless of your individual situation, each of you will find your path. If you are genuinely willing to reach out for and to accept help, put forth unimaginable personal effort, and continue to look ahead at what possibilities await, you will reach a better—and perhaps unexpected—place. You, too, have the ability to regain your confidence, abandon your hopelessness, and realize that you are not a woman to be tossed aside and forgotten. You are a woman capable and worthy of great things. Let yourself remain open to new opportunities and receptive to new connections. Let yourself enjoy those things, whatever they may be. If I could find my way back, you can do the same.

Acknowledgments

There are so many to whom I owe my thanks and appreciation for this book and for my very survival, especially the friends and family, distant and near, who were as shocked and shattered as I but still offered their unwavering love, support, and encouragement to help me remain strong in the face of unimagined adversity; who reminded me to find the good in every day and to keep moving forward; who believed in my courage and fortitude when I was unable to believe in myself.

To my readers who muddled through the initial draft of this work, constantly cheering me on and assuring me that the story had merit and deserved a wider audience, and to my dear friend Mary-Ann, who not only read and reread each word, word change, and update but also offered unwavering, immediate, and insightful support and wisdom throughout this journey: without your steadfast assistance, gentle prodding, and kind words, I could never have accomplished my goal. To those who generously allowed the use of their quotes and offered their encouragement and assistance for this book: your selfless backing and reassurance allowed me to believe that I might indeed be able to see this project through.

Thanks to Brooke Warner, who not only accepted my work as worthy of publication but had a talented and professional organization in place to guide the manuscript, and this inexperienced author, through the editing and publishing process while providing all of the necessary support to ensure success. And who introduced me to Annie Tucker, the wonderful and talented editor who propelled me forward, step by step and word by word, encouraging me to make each scene and moment in this book as real for my readers as it was for me. Thank you, Annie, for helping my story to become all that you knew it could be, and even more than I could have imagined.

And to every person, familiar or stranger, professional and nonprofessional, who crossed my path and selflessly offered support, guidance, and a caring word or gesture: know that with even the smallest acts of unexpected kindness, you provided the strength and determination I needed at any given moment to persevere, grow, and thrive. All were yet another confirmation that we are interconnected and here to help one another along life's journey. For all, I will forever be truly indebted and grateful.

ABOUT THE AUTHOR

Photo credit: Shelby Sieg

For thirty years, Kathryn Taylor taught life's most important lessons to elementary-school children as a public-school teacher. In her retirement, she realized that she had valuable wisdom and experiences to share with adults—specifically, women experiencing "gray divorce." Divorced once at forty, Taylor spent most of her adult life as a single working mother and dedicated herself to raising her two daughters. She had proven herself a strong, loving, independent woman, so she was surprised when she found herself struggling to deal with her second divorce. Through writing this, her first book, she uncovered the strong, loving, independent woman that remained, and it is her hope that her story helps women in similar circumstances recover their own strength and self-love. She and Lucy live near Charleston, South Carolina.

Visit www.kathryntaylorbooks.com.

SELECTED TITLES FROM SHE WRITES PRESS

She Writes Press is an independent publishing company
founded to serve women writers everywhere.
Visit us at www.shewritespress.com.

Loveyoubye: Holding Fast, Letting Go, And Then There's The Dog by
Rossandra White. $16.95, 978-1-938314-50-6. A soul-searching
memoir detailing the painful, but ultimately liberating, disintegration
of a twenty-five-year marriage.

The Full Catastrophe: A Memoir by Karen Elizabeth Lee. $16.95,
978-1-63152-024-2. The story of a well educated, professional
woman who, after marrying the wrong kind of man—twice—finally
resurrects her life.

The Sportscaster's Daughter: A Memoir by Cindi Michael. $16.95,
978-1-63152-107-2. Despite being disowned by her father—
sportscaster George Michael, said to be the man who inspired ESPN's
SportsCenter—Cindi Michael manages financially and heals
emotionally, ultimately finding confidence from within.

There Was a Fire Here: A Memoir by Risa Nye. $16.95,
978-1-63152-045-7. After a devastating firestorm destroys Risa Nye's
Oakland, California home and neighborhood, she has to dig deep to
discover her inner strength and resilience.

Filling Her Shoes: Memoir of an Inherited Family by Betsy Graziani
Fasbinder. $16.95, 978-1-63152-198-0. A "sweet-bitter" story of how,
with tenderness as their guide, a family formed in the wake of loss
and learned that joy and grief can be entwined cohabitants in our lives.

*Falling Together: How to Find Balance, Joy, and Meaningful Change When
Your Life Seems to be Falling Apart* by Donna Cardillo. $16.95,
978-1-63152-077-8. A funny, big-hearted self-help memoir that
tackles divorce, caregiving, burnout, major illness, fears, and low
self-esteem—and explores the renewal that comes when we are able
to meet these challenges with courage.